First World War

and Army of Occupation

War Diary

France, Belgium and Germany

58 DIVISION
Divisional Troops
503 Field Company Royal Engineers
23 January 1917 - 31 May 1919

WO95/2996/2

The Naval & Military Press Ltd
www.nmarchive.com
Published in association with The National Archives

Published by

The Naval & Military Press Ltd

Unit 10 Ridgewood Industrial Park,
Uckfield, East Sussex,
TN22 5QE England
Tel: +44 (0) 1825 749494

www.naval-military-press.com
www.nmarchive.com

This diary has been reprinted in facsimile from the original. Any imperfections are inevitably reproduced and the quality may fall short of modern type and cartographic standards.

Contents

Document type	Place/Title	Date From	Date To
Heading	WO95/2996/2		
War Diary	Southampton	23/01/1917	23/01/1917
War Diary	Le Havre France	24/01/1917	24/01/1917
War Diary	Point 3 Le Havre	25/01/1917	25/01/1917
War Diary	Frevent (Ref Map-Lens 3D.5.3)	26/01/1917	26/01/1917
War Diary	Barly	28/01/1917	28/01/1917
Heading	War Diary Of 503rd (Wessex) Field Coy R.E. February 1917 Vol 2		
War Diary	Ivergny	02/02/1917	20/02/1917
War Diary	Pas	20/02/1917	20/02/1917
War Diary	Ivergny	22/02/1917	22/02/1917
War Diary	Lucheux	24/02/1917	24/02/1917
War Diary	Le Souich	24/02/1917	24/02/1917
War Diary	Grosville	25/02/1917	25/02/1917
Heading	War Diary Of 503rd (Wessex) Field Co. RE From 26th February 1917 To 26th March 1917 Vol		
War Diary	Grosville	26/02/1917	01/03/1917
War Diary	Fermont	02/03/1917	20/03/1917
War Diary	Ficheux	20/03/1917	20/03/1917
War Diary	Fermont	21/03/1917	21/03/1917
War Diary	Ficheux	21/03/1917	21/03/1917
War Diary	Fermont	22/03/1917	22/03/1917
War Diary	Boiry St Martin	22/03/1917	23/03/1917
War Diary	Bienvillers	23/03/1917	23/03/1917
War Diary	Boiry St Martin	24/03/1917	24/03/1917
War Diary	Bienvillers	24/03/1917	24/03/1917
War Diary	Boiry St Martin	25/03/1917	25/03/1917
War Diary	Bienvillers	25/03/1917	25/03/1917
War Diary	Boiry St Martin	26/03/1917	26/03/1917
War Diary	Bienvillers	26/03/1917	26/03/1917
Heading	War Diary Of 503rd (Wessex) Field Co. RE From 27th March 1917 To 26th April 1917		
War Diary	Halloy	27/03/1917	01/04/1917
War Diary	Occoches	02/04/1917	02/04/1917
War Diary	Rougefay	03/04/1917	05/04/1917
War Diary	Bus Le Artois	06/04/1917	06/04/1917
War Diary	Doullens	06/04/1917	06/04/1917
War Diary	Bus Le Artois	07/04/1917	08/04/1917
War Diary	Irles	09/04/1917	10/04/1917
War Diary	Bihucourt	11/04/1917	23/04/1917
War Diary	Mory	23/04/1917	23/04/1917
War Diary	Bihucourt	24/04/1917	24/04/1917
War Diary	Mory	24/04/1917	24/04/1917
War Diary	Bihucourt	25/04/1917	25/04/1917
War Diary	Mory	25/04/1917	25/04/1917
War Diary	Bihucourt	26/04/1917	26/04/1917
War Diary	Mory	27/04/1917	27/04/1917
War Diary	Bihucourt	27/04/1917	27/04/1917
War Diary	Mory	28/04/1917	28/04/1917
War Diary	Bihucourt	28/04/1917	28/04/1917

War Diary	Mory	29/04/1917	29/04/1917
War Diary	Bihucourt	29/04/1917	29/04/1917
War Diary	Mory	30/04/1917	30/04/1917
War Diary	Bihucourt	30/04/1917	30/04/1917
War Diary	Mory	01/05/1917	01/05/1917
War Diary	Bihucourt	01/05/1917	01/05/1917
War Diary	Mory	02/05/1917	02/05/1917
War Diary	Bihucourt	02/05/1917	02/05/1917
War Diary	Mory	03/05/1917	03/05/1917
War Diary	Bihucourt	03/05/1917	03/05/1917
War Diary	Mory	04/05/1917	04/05/1917
War Diary	Bihucourt	04/05/1917	04/05/1917
War Diary	Mory	04/05/1917	04/05/1917
War Diary	Vraucourt	05/05/1917	02/06/1917
War Diary	Mory	03/06/1917	24/06/1917
War Diary	Logeast Wood (57c G 2c 3.7)	25/06/1917	05/07/1917
War Diary	Bancourt (H 36 Central)	06/07/1917	06/07/1917
War Diary	Ytres	07/07/1917	07/07/1917
War Diary	Havrin Court Wood (P 18 Central)	08/07/1917	09/07/1917
War Diary	Ref Map 57c Havrincourt Wood	10/07/1917	16/07/1917
War Diary	Ruyalcourt	17/07/1917	19/07/1917
War Diary	Ref Map 57c 1/20000 Ruyalcourt	20/07/1917	27/07/1917
War Diary	Fosseux Lens II G 3.8.1	28/07/1917	30/07/1917
War Diary	H 32 C.5.3 (Sheet 51b)	31/07/1917	20/08/1917
War Diary	Duisans L7.as 90 51.c 1/10000	20/08/1917	25/08/1917
War Diary	Ref Map Sheet 28. N.W. G6.a.5.8.	26/08/1917	29/08/1917
War Diary	C25.d.3.5	29/08/1917	31/08/1917
War Diary	Ref Map Sheet 28 NW 1/20000 C25.d 3.5	01/09/1917	19/09/1917
War Diary	Reference Map Sheet 28 NW C22.b.7.0.	20/09/1917	27/09/1917
War Diary	A22 B 8.4.	28/09/1917	30/09/1917
War Diary	Ref Map Sheet 28 N.W. 1/20000 A22 B 8.4	01/10/1917	01/10/1917
War Diary	Lostrat (2A 2.1)	02/10/1917	16/10/1917
War Diary	Hazebrouck 1/10000 Lostrat 2A 2.1	17/10/1917	20/10/1917
War Diary	Hospital Farm	21/10/1917	25/10/1917
War Diary	Caledonia Trench C15 A 7.6	26/10/1917	31/10/1917
War Diary	Reference Map Sheet 28 N.W. 1/20000 Caledonia Trench C15. A 7.6.	01/11/1917	15/11/1917
War Diary	CB. C.3.3	16/11/1917	17/11/1917
War Diary	Sheet 27.N.W. E7a. 8.8	18/11/1917	27/11/1917
War Diary	Hazebrouck Sheet 5.A Samette (4 B 5.4.)	28/11/1917	28/11/1917
War Diary	Longueville (Calais Sheet 1/100000 4 E 5.8)	29/11/1917	04/12/1917
War Diary	Samette	05/12/1917	06/12/1917
War Diary	Canal Bank 2K4.8. Sheet 5 A	07/12/1917	10/12/1917
War Diary	Ref Map Hazebrouck Canal Bank 2k 4.8.	11/12/1917	31/12/1917
War Diary	Ref Map Sheet 5.A. Canal Bank 2.K 4.8	01/01/1918	16/01/1918
War Diary	Proven (Sheet 27, E12 D 2.7)	17/01/1918	20/01/1918
War Diary	Aubigny (Amiens Sheet 2F.7.8)	21/01/1918	23/01/1918
War Diary	Rosieres (3.I.5.8.)	24/01/1918	24/01/1918
War Diary	Rove (4.J.5.4.)	25/01/1918	25/01/1918
War Diary	Ognolles 4.K.95.40	26/01/1918	26/01/1918
War Diary	Neuplieux (St Quentin Sheet 5. B 9.5)	27/01/1918	02/02/1918
War Diary	Viry Noureuil Sheet 70 D.A 10 A 3.5.)	03/02/1918	15/02/1918
War Diary	Viry Noureuil	16/02/1918	28/02/1918
War Diary	Viry Noureuil (Sheet 70 D A 16a 1.7.)	01/03/1918	23/03/1918
War Diary	Besme R 14 B 9.5.	24/03/1918	31/03/1918
Heading	War Diary 503rd Field Company, R.E. April 1918		

War Diary	Besme R4 B 9.5	01/04/1918	01/04/1918
War Diary	Bleqancourt	02/04/1918	02/04/1918
War Diary	Le Mesnil	03/04/1918	03/04/1918
War Diary	Ambleny	04/04/1918	04/04/1918
War Diary	Dommiers	05/04/1918	05/04/1918
War Diary	2 E 5.3 Amiens Sheet	06/04/1918	18/04/1918
War Diary	1/2 Miles East Of Cagny At M 36d 5.2. (Sheet 62D)	19/04/1918	27/04/1918
War Diary	Coulonvillers (Lens.5A.1.7)	28/04/1918	30/04/1918
Heading	War Diary Of 503rd Field Coy R.E From 1-5-18 To 31-5-18 Vol 17		
War Diary	Coulenvillers (Lens 5.A1.7)	01/05/1918	05/05/1918
War Diary	Braizieux	06/05/1918	15/05/1918
War Diary	V 20 D 4.4.	16/05/1918	22/05/1918
War Diary	Warloy U 24 B.7.8	23/05/1918	28/05/1918
War Diary	C 5 B 7.8.	29/05/1918	31/05/1918
Heading	War Diary Of 503rd (Wessex) Field Coy RE For Period 1-6-18 To 30-6-18 Vol XVII		
War Diary	C B 7.8.	01/06/1918	05/06/1918
War Diary	B 9 A. 3.3.	06/06/1918	10/06/1918
War Diary	P 20 C.7.3 (62 D)	11/06/1918	19/06/1918
War Diary	C 11d 1.7	20/06/1918	28/06/1918
War Diary	C A 6.4	29/06/1918	30/06/1918
Heading	War Diary Of 503rd (Wessex) Field Co. R.E. For Period 1-7-18 To 31-7-18 Vol XVIII		
War Diary	C 5 A.6.4.	01/07/1918	31/07/1918
Heading	58th Divl. Engineers 503rd Field Company, Royal Engineers, August 1918		
War Diary	C 5.a.6.5	01/08/1918	03/08/1918
War Diary	I 15 A.5.5.62 D	04/08/1918	30/08/1918
War Diary	A 25.d.4.2. (62.c)	31/08/1918	31/08/1918
Heading	War Diary Of 503rd (Wessex) Field Coy R.E. (T) For Period 1-9-18 To 30-9-18 Vol XIX		
War Diary	A.25 D.4.2.	01/09/1918	04/09/1918
War Diary	B 21 A.5.6.	05/09/1918	07/09/1918
War Diary	Moislains	08/09/1918	12/09/1918
War Diary	Nurlu	13/09/1918	27/09/1918
War Diary	Camblain L'Abbe	28/09/1918	30/09/1918
Heading	War Diary Of 503rd Field Coy R.E. For Period 1-10-18 To 31-10-18 Vol XXII		
War Diary	Ablain St Nazaire	01/10/1918	04/10/1918
War Diary	Angres	05/10/1918	08/10/1918
War Diary	Cite St Pierre	09/10/1918	13/10/1918
War Diary	Cite Du Grand Conde	14/10/1918	15/10/1918
War Diary	Courrieres	16/10/1918	16/10/1918
War Diary	Faumont	18/10/1918	18/10/1918
War Diary	La Planque	19/10/1918	19/10/1918
War Diary	Aix	20/10/1918	20/10/1918
War Diary	Rumegies	21/10/1918	09/11/1918
War Diary	Weirs	10/11/1918	10/11/1918
War Diary	Ecacheries	11/11/1918	14/11/1918
War Diary	Beloeil	15/11/1918	29/11/1918
War Diary	Weirs	30/11/1918	30/11/1918
Heading	War Diary Of 503rd Field Company R.E. For The Period 1.11.18 To 30.11.18		
War Diary	Wiers	01/12/1918	31/12/1918
Heading	503rd Coy RE Vol 25		

War Diary	Wiers	10/02/1919	21/02/1919
War Diary	Leuze	22/02/1919	28/02/1919
War Diary	Leuze	01/03/1919	31/05/1919

58 DW

Vol 1

558

Army Form C. 2118.

Instructions regarding War Diaries and Intelligence Summaries are contained in F. S. Regs., Part II. and the Staff Manual respectively. Title pages will be prepared in manuscript.

WAR DIARY
or
~~INTELLIGENCE SUMMARY.~~
(Erase heading not required.)

503rd (Wessex) Fd: Co: R.E.

Hour, Date, Place	Summary of Events and Information	Remarks and references to Appendices
4·15 p.m. 23rd January 1917. SOUTHAMPTON	Company embarked.	b/b.
12·30 p.m. 24th January 1917. LE HAVRE. FRANCE	Company disembarked and marched to DOCKS REST CAMP. LE HAVRE for night.	b/b.
8·30 am. 25th January 1917. Point 3. LE HAVRE	Company entrained.	b/b.
2·0 p.m. 26th January 1917. FRÉVENT (Reg Map:- LENS. 3D.5.3)	Company detrained and marched to BARLY (LENS 4D 3.4) Billeted.	b/b.
11·0 am. 28th January 1917. BARLY	Company marched to IVERGNY (LENS 4E.7.8). – Billeted – Work on water supply, – erecting Huts &c.	b/b.

[illegible] Major
Commdg. 503rd Fd. Co. R.E.

(73989) W4141—463. 400,000. 9/14. H.&J.Ltd. Forms/C. 2118/10.

· CONFIDENTIAL ·

War Diary of 503rd (Wessex) Field Coy R.E.
February 1917.

Vol 2

58

Instructions regarding War Diaries and Intelligence Summaries are contained in F. S. Regs., Part II. and the Staff Manual respectively. Title pages will be prepared in manuscript.

WAR DIARY
or
~~INTELLIGENCE SUMMARY.~~
(*Erase heading not required.*)

Army Form C. 2118.

Hour, Date, Place	Summary of Events and Information	Remarks and references to Appendices
11 am. 2nd February 1917. IVERGNY	No 4 Section proceeded to PAS (LENS 5F 99) for the purpose of erecting huts &c.	
2 p.m. 2nd February 1917 IVERGNY	No 3 Section proceeded to LUCHEUX (LENS 4E9A) for the purpose of erecting huts &c.	
2.30pm 2nd February 1917. IVERGNY.	No 1. Section proceeded to LE SOUICH (LENS 4E 56) for the purpose of erecting huts &c.	
9.30am 20th February 1917. IVERGNY.	Headquarters with all vehicles proceeded by march route to LE FERMONT (LENS. 4I4.8) via LAHERLIÉRE (LENS 4G75) to be attached to 57th Fd. Co. R.E. preparatory to taking over work on front line. All horses and vehicles remaining at LAHERLIÉRE.	
1 p.m 20th February 1917 PAS.	No. 4 Section proceeded by route march to GROSVILLE (LENS. 4I 28) via GAUDIEMPRE - LA CAUCHIE - BAILLEUMONT for work on front line. &c	
10.30 am. 22nd February 1917 IVERGNY	No. 2 Section proceeded by march route to GROSVILLE via LAHERLIÉRE for work on front line &c	
10.30 am. 24th February 1917 LUCHEUX	No 3. Section proceeded by march route to GROSVILLE via MONDICOURT - DOULLENS - ARRAS ROAD for work on front line &c	
11.15 am 24th February 1917. LE SOUICH	No 1 Section proceeded by march route to GROSVILLE. via MONDICOURT - DOULLENS - ARRAS ROAD for work on front line &c	
9 am. 25th February 1917 GROSVILLE	Took over work from 546 Fd. Co. R.E. on front line - From FOREST STREET to ENGINEER STREET - DYKE STREET inclusive (Ref Map FICHEUX 51c SE. & 51b S.W (parts of) 1/10.000) also BRETENCOURT water supply.	

(73989) W4141—463. 400,000. 9/14. H.&J.Ltd. Forms/C. 2118/10.

503RD
(WESSEX)
FIELD COMPANY, R.E.
No.
Date.

Vol

CONFIDENTIAL

WAR DIARY

of

503rd (WESSEX) FIELD CO. R.E.

From:- 26th February 1917. To:- 26th March 1917.

VOL:-

Instructions regarding War Diaries and Intelligence Summaries are contained in F. S. Regs., Part II. and the Staff Manual respectively. Title pages will be prepared in manuscript.

WAR DIARY or ~~INTELLIGENCE~~ SUMMARY.

(*Erase heading not required.*)

503RD (WESSEX) FIELD COMPANY, R.E.
No.........
Date.........

Army Form C. 2118.

Hour, Date, Place	Summary of Events and Information	Remarks and references to Appendices
Reference Map:- FICHEUX. 51c S.E. & 51b S.W. (parts of) 1/10000.		
26th FEBRUARY 1917:- GROSVILLE	No 1. Section. Working on Strong Points and Dug Outs with 57th Field Co: RE. " 2 " -do- -do- -do- " 3 " -do- -do- -do- " 4 " Constructing Strong Points at R33a65 (SUNKEN ROAD POST) R27d3005 (QUARRY POST) and repairing burst pipes of BRETENCOURT WATER SCHEME.	
27th FEBRUARY 1917.	No 1. Section. As 26th February 1917. " 2 " -do- " 3 " -do- " 4 " Revetting C.T's QUARRY STREET & ENGINEER STREET. and work on BRETENCOURT water supply.	
28th FEBRUARY 1917:-	Work taken over from 57th Field Co: RE. on Front Line &c - From GAME STREET (exclusive) to FOREST STREET. and BRIGADE HD. QRS Dug Out at Chateau (R26d99). No 1 Section. Dug Out Brigade Hd Qrs R26d99. " 2 " Dug Out at FENCHURCH POST R24c89. " 3 " Dug Out at FISHERGATE POST R28b11. " 4 " Revetting CT's LITTLE BRIDGE STREET and QUARRY STREET and work on BRETENCOURT water supply.	
9am 1st MARCH 1917:- GROSVILLE.	Nos: 1.2.3 & 4 Sections moved to FERMONT and took over billets vacated by 57th Field Co: RE. No 1. Section Dug Outs at Brigade Hd Qrs (R26d 99) and FENCHURCH POST (R24c89) " 2 " Dug Outs at R23c89. (CHANCERY LANE) and FROG STREET (R24c21) " 3 " Dug Out at FISHERGATE POST (R28b11.) " 4 " Revetting ENGINEER STREET and repairing burst pipes BRETENCOURT water supply.	

(73989) W4141—463. 400,000. 9/14. H.&J.Ltd. Forms/C. 2118/10.

Instructions regarding War Diaries and Intelligence Summaries are contained in F. S. Regs., Part II. and the Staff Manual respectively. Title pages will be prepared in manuscript.

WAR DIARY
or
~~INTELLIGENCE SUMMARY.~~
(Erase heading not required.)

503RD (WESSEX) FIELD COMPANY, R.E.
No.
Date.

Army Form C. 2118.

Hour, Date, Place	Summary of Events and Information	Remarks and references to Appendices
Reference Map:- FICHEUX 51cSE & 51bSW (parts of) 1/10.000.		
2nd MARCH 1917. FERMONT.	No 1 Section. STRONG Points at R24c 8.9. (FENCHURCH POST) and M. 19b 13. FLEET POST. – Shelter at M 19c 17. (FENCHURCH STREET at Front Line) " 2 " STRONG Point at R29b 47 (FRENCH POST) – Shelter at R 29a 6570 (FOLLY LANE at Front Line) – Dug Out at R23c 89 (CHANCERY LANE) " 3 " Dug Out at R28b 11. (FISHERGATE POST) – Revetting C.T. FINE STREET. " 4 " As on 1st March 1917. Reinforcement of 1 Sapper (No 459705 Sapper Bond E.)	[signature] Capt
3rd MARCH 1917:- FERMONT.	No 1. Section. Strong Points at R24d 1558 (FARM POST) and as on 2nd March 1917 " 2 " Strong Points at R29b 47. (FRENCH STREET) – R23d 84 (FRANCIS STREET) – R 29a 2510. (FOLLY POST) " 3 " Strong Points at R28b11. (FISHERGATE POST) – R 28c 3045 (MARTINETS POST) – R28a 52 (CHANCERY POST) – Dug Outs at R29c 4045 (Front line at FINE STREET) and R28d0500 (Front) line at FOREST STREET. " 4 " As on 2nd March 1917:- and revetting SUNKEN ROAD & QUARRY STREET.	[signature] Capt
4th MARCH 1917:- FERMONT.	Inspection of Company by O.C. – Baths &c – One sapper wounded – (No 504555 Sapper Pearce W.H.)	[signature] Capt
5th MARCH 1917. FERMONT.	No. 1 Section. As on 3rd March 1917. – " 2 " -do- -do- and Dug Out at R 23c 89. (CHANCERY LANE) " 3 " -do- -do- " 4 " -do- -do-.	[signature] Capt

(73989) W4141—463. 400,000. 9/14. H.&J.Ltd. Forms/C. 2118/10.

* Instructions regarding War Diaries and Intelligence Summaries are contained in F. S. Regs., Part II. and the Staff Manual respectively. Title pages will be prepared in manuscript.

WAR DIARY

~~or~~

~~INTELLIGENCE SUMMARY.~~

(Erase heading not required.)

503RD (WESSEX) FIELD COMPANY, R.E.
No.........
Date.........

Army Form C. 2118.

Hour, Date, Place	Summary of Events and Information	Remarks and references to Appendices
Reference Map :- FICHEUX :- 51c SE & 51b S.W (parts of) 1/10.000		
6th MARCH 1917. FERMONT.	No. 1 Section. As on 5th March 1917. " 2 " -do- -do- " 3 " -do- -do- " 4 " -do- -do- and Strong point at R27d 3005 (QUARRY POST).	[signature] Capt
7th MARCH 1917. FERMONT.	No 1. Section. As on 6th March 1917. " 2 " -do- -do- " 3 " Strong points at R32d 2859. (HEDGES POST) - R32c 3538 (CHURCH POST) " 4 " Strong points at R27d 3005 (QUARRY POST) & R33a G5 (SUNKEN ROAD POST) and BRETENCOURT WATER SCHEME Work taken over from 511th Fd Co R.E on trenches from ENGINEER STREET - DYKE STREET to PARK STREET (exclusive)	[signature] Capt
8th MARCH 1917 FERMONT.	No. 1 Section. As on 7th March 1917. " 2 " -do- -do- " 3 " -do- -do- and Strong Point at R31c 91. (BOUNDARY POST) " 4 " -do- -do- and revetting C.T.'s QUARRY STREET & ENGINEER STREET	[signature] Capt.
9th MARCH 1917. FERMONT.	No. 1. Section. As on 8th March 1917 and strong point at R23d 84 (FRANCIS POST). " 2 " -do- -do- excluding strong point at R23d 84 (FRANCIS POST). " 3 " -do- -do- " 4 " -do- -do-	[signature] Capt.
10th MARCH 1917. FERMONT	No. 1 Section. As on 9th March 1917. " 2 " -do- -do- " 3 " -do- -do- " 4 " -do- -do- One mounted N.C.O killed (No 504303 L/Corpl Stockham T)	[signature] Capt

Instructions regarding War Diaries and Intelligence Summaries are contained in F. S. Regs., Part II. and the Staff Manual respectively. Title pages will be prepared in manuscript.

WAR DIARY
or
~~INTELLIGENCE SUMMARY.~~

(*Erase heading not required.*)

503RD (WESSEX) FIELD COMPANY, R.E.
No.........
Date.........

Army Form C. 2118.

Reference Map.. FICHEUX 51c SE & 51b SW (parts of) 1/10,000

Hour, Date, Place	Summary of Events and Information	Remarks and references to Appendices
11th MARCH 1917. FERMONT.	Inspection of Company by O.C. – Baths &c. –	[signature] Capt.
12th MARCH 1917. FERMONT.	No. 1. Section. As on 10th MARCH 1917. " 2 " -do- -do- " 3 " Strong points at R32d 2859 (HEDGES POST) – R32c 3538 (CHURCH POST) and R33c 7525 (OSIER POST). " 4 " As on 10th March 1917. DUG OUT at R26d 99. (BRIGADE HEAD QUARTERS.	[signature] Capt.
13th MARCH 1917. FERMONT.	No: 1. Section. As on 12th March 1917 " 2 " -do- -do- " 3 " -do- -do- " 4 " -do- -do- Dug Out at R26d 99. (BRIGADE HEAD QUARTERS)	[signature] Capt.
14th MARCH 1917. FERMONT.	No: 1. Section. As on 13th March 1917 " 2 " -do- -do- " 3 " -do- -do- " 4 " -do- -do- Dug Out at R26d 99. (BRIGADE HEAD QUARTERS). One sapper wounded (No 504360 Sapper Jennings W.E)	[signature] Capt.
15th MARCH 1917. FERMONT.	No. 1. Section. As on 14th March 1917 " 2 " -do- -do- " 3 " -do- -do- " 4 " -do- -do- Dug Out at R26d 99 (BRIGADE HEAD QUARTERS)	[signature] Capt.

(73989) W4141—463. 400,000. 9/14. H.&J.Ltd. Forms/C. 2118/10.

Instructions regarding War Diaries and Intelligence Summaries are contained in F. S. Regs., Part II. and the Staff Manual respectively. Title pages will be prepared in manuscript.

WAR DIARY

~~or~~

~~INTELLIGENCE SUMMARY.~~

(Erase heading not required.)

Army Form C. 2118.

Reference Map:- FICHEUX:- 51cSE & 51bSW (parts of) 1/10.000.

Hour, Date, Place	Summary of Events and Information	Remarks and references to Appendices
16th March 1917. FERMONT.	No. 1. Section. As on 15th March 1917. " 2. " -do- -do- " 3 " -do- -do- " 4 " -do- -do- Dug Out at R26d 99. (BRIGADE HEAD QUARTERS).	[signature] Capt
17th March 1917. FERMONT.	No. 1. Section. As on 16th March 1917. " 2 " -do- -do- " 3 " -do- -do- " 4 " -do- -do- Dug Out at R26d 99 (BRIGADE HEAD QUARTERS)	[signature] Capt
18th March 1917. FERMONT.	No 1. Section. } " 2 " } Clearing barricades - filling in trenches &c on WAILLY - FICHEUX Road. " 3 " -do- -do- -do- BELLACOURT - RANSART Road. " 4 " -do- -do- -do- BRETENCOURT - BLAIRVILLE Road.	[signature] Capt
19th March 1917. FERMONT.	No 1 Section, " 2 " " 3 " " 4 " } Road making WAILLY - FICHEUX ROAD.	
9 am. 19th March 1917. FERMONT.	No. 4 Section proceeded to FICHEUX and took up forward billets:- (CRE's 58th Division Operation Order No. 13. dated 18th March 1917) " " Erecting temporary bridges for pack transport at S11c 88 & S12a 0055. (Ref. Map. BOISLEUX 51bSW(3) 1/10,000)	[signature] Capt
20th March 1917. FERMONT	No 1 Sections " 2 " " 3 " } Road making WAILLY - FICHEUX ROAD.	
20th March 1917. FICHEUX	No 4 Section Road making FICHEUX - BOISLEUX ROAD.	[signature] Capt

Instructions regarding War Diaries and Intelligence Summaries are contained in F. S. Regs., Part II. and the Staff Manual respectively. Title pages will be prepared in manuscript.

WAR DIARY

~~or~~

~~INTELLIGENCE SUMMARY.~~

(Erase heading not required.)

503RD (WESSEX) FIELD COMPANY, R.E.
No.........
Date.........

Army Form C. 2118.

Hour, Date, Place	Summary of Events and Information	Remarks and references to Appendices
Reference Map:- BOISLEUX. 51bS.W.3 1/10,000.		
21st March 1917. FERMONT	No. 1 Section, 2 " , 3 " } Road making WAILLY - FICHEUX ROAD.	
21st March 1917. FICHEUX	" 4 " Road making FICHEUX - BOISLEUX Road.	[signature] Capt
8am 22nd March 1917. FERMONT } FICHEUX	No. 1 Section, " 3 ", " 4 " } Proceeded to BOIRY ST MARTIN and took up forward billets. } C.R.E's 58th Division Operation Order No. 15 dated 21:3:17	
10 am 22nd March 1917. FERMONT	Headquarters, No. 2 Section } Proceeded to BIENVILLERS (LENS. (1/100,000) 4 H 51) and billeted.	
22nd March 1917. BOIRY ST MARTIN.	No. 1 Section, " 3 ", " 4 " } Repairing roads at { S 19b 46. S 14a 7525. S 14c 68.	[signature] Capt
23rd March 1917. BOIRY ST MARTIN.	No. 1 Section, " 3 " } Repairing roads at { S 19b 46, S 14c 68. " 4 " Repairing roadway at S 11c 3585 and preparing materials for bridge at S 11c 88.	
23rd March 1917. BIENVILLERS.	No. 2 Section. Repairing roadway &c at BIENVILLERS.	[signature] Capt
24th March 1917. BOIRY ST MARTIN	No. 1 Section, " 3 " } Repairing roadway at S19b46. " 4 " Repairing roadway at S11c3585 and erecting trestles for bridge at S11c88.	
24th March 1917. BIENVILLERS.	No. 2 Section. Repairing roadway &c at BIENVILLERS.	[signature] Capt

(73989) W4141—463. 400,000. 9/14. H.&J.Ltd. Forms/C. 2118/10.

Instructions regarding War Diaries and Intelligence Summaries are contained in F. S. Regs., Part II. and the Staff Manual respectively. Title pages will be prepared in manuscript.

WAR DIARY

or

~~INTELLIGENCE~~ SUMMARY.

(Erase heading not required.)

503RD (WESSEX) FIELD COMPANY, R.E.
No.
Date.

Army Form C. 2118.

Hour, Date, Place	Summary of Events and Information	Remarks and references to Appendices
Reference Map:- BOISLEUX 51SW 3 1/10.000.		
25th March 1917. BOIRY ST MARTIN.	No: 1 Section. " 3 " " 4 " } As on 24th March 1917.	
25th March 1917. BIENVILLERS	" 2 " -do- -do-	[signature] Capt.
9 am. 26th March 1917. BOIRY ST MARTIN	No: 1 Section " 3 " " 4 " } Proceeded by march route to HALLOY (LENS 11. 5F28. 1/100000) via POMMIER - HUMBERCAMP - GAUDIEMPRE - PAS.	CRE's 58th Division Operation Order No. 16. dated 25th March 1917
10 am 26th March 1917. BIENVILLERS	Headquarters. No: 2 Section } -do- -do- -do-	
	All work in hand handed over to 97th Field Co: RE.	[signature] Capt.

(73989) W4141—463. 400,000. 9/14. H.&J.Ltd. Forms/C. 2118/10.

Vol 4

CONFIDENTIAL

WAR DIARY

OF

503rd (WESSEX) FIELD CO: R.E.

From. 27th March 1917. To: 26th April 1917.

Instructions regarding War Diaries and Intelligence Summaries are contained in F. S. Regs., Part II. and the Staff Manual respectively. Title pages will be prepared in manuscript.

WAR DIARY
or
~~INTELLIGENCE SUMMARY.~~
(*Erase heading not required.*)

Army Form C. 2118.

Hour, Date, Place	Summary of Events and Information	Remarks and references to Appendices
Reference Map:- LENS 11. 1/100.000		
27th March 1917. HALLOY.	Checking equipment, stores &c:- cleaning vehicles.	[signature]
28th March 1917 to 31st March 1917. HALLOY.	Training.	[signature]
11 am. 1st April 1917 HALLOY.	Company proceeded by march route to OCCOCHES (LENS. 4D. 21. 1/100,000) and billeted. (via DOULLENS - RISQUETOUT) (175th Infantry Brigade Order No 10)	[signature]
10 am 2nd April 1917. OCCOCHES.	Company proceeded by march route to ROUGEFAY (LENS. 3C.13. 1/100.000) and billeted (via FROHEN - WAVANS - NOEUX) 175th Infantry Brigade Order No 11)	[signature]
3rd April 1917. ROUGEFAY.	Cleaning billets &c.	[signature]
4th April 1917. ROUGEFAY	Inspection of Company by O.C.	[signature]

Instructions regarding War Diaries and Intelligence Summaries are contained in F. S. Regs., Part II. and the Staff Manual respectively. Title pages will be prepared in manuscript.

WAR DIARY
or
~~INTELLIGENCE SUMMARY.~~

(Erase heading not required.)

Army Form C. 2118.

Place	Date	Hour	Summary of Events and Information	Remarks and references to Appendices
Reference Map:-		LENS	11. 1/100.000.	
ROUGEFAY	5:4:17	9.30 am	Company dismounted proceeded by motor bus to BUS-LES-ARTOIS (4H 6.3) and took up quarters in huts. Company Transport proceeded by march route to DOULLENS (5E.1.8.) and billeted	175 Infy Brigade Operation Order No.12 4:4:17
BUS-LE-ARTOIS	6:4:17		Cleaning huts &c.	
DOULLENS	6:4:17	8.30 am	Company transport proceeded by march route to BUS-LES-ARTOIS (4H6.3) and joined Company in Hutment Camp	
BUS-LE-ARTOIS	7:4:17		Cleaning Camp &c.	
BUS-LE ARTOIS	8:4:17	9. am	Company proceeded by march route to IRLES (5J.05.25) and billeted. (175 Infy. Bgde. Operation Order No.13. 7.4.17.)	
IRLES.	9:4:17		Company erecting shelters &c.	
-do-	10:4:17	2 p.m.	Company proceeded by march route, and encamped on BIHUCOURT-SAPIGNIES road at G.12 c.7.5 (Sheet 57c 1/40000)	
BIHUCOURT	11:4:17	5 am.	No. 1 Section:- Diversion of roadway to filling point of Water Transport. No 4 Section:- Standings and approaches to water troughs (36 a 1.9) (Sheet 57c 1/40.000)	
-do-	11:4:17	1 p.m.	" 2 " -do- -do- " 3 " -do- -do-	
-do-	12:4:17	5. am.	Nos: 1 & 4 Sections:- as on 11:4:1917.	
		1 pm	" 2 & 3 " -do-	
-do-	13:4:17	5 am	" 1 & 4 Sections -do-	
		1 pm	" 2 & 3 " -do-	
-do-	14:4:17	5 am	" 1 & 4 " -do-	
		1 pm.	" 2 & 3 " -do-	

T2134. Wt. W708—776. 500000. 4/15. Sir J. C. & S.

Instructions regarding War Diaries and Intelligence Summaries are contained in F. S. Regs., Part II. and the Staff Manual respectively. Title pages will be prepared in manuscript.

WAR DIARY

~~or~~

~~INTELLIGENCE SUMMARY.~~

(Erase heading not required.)

Army Form C. 2118.

Place	Date	Hour	Summary of Events and Information	Remarks and references to Appendices
Reference Map: LENS 11. 1/100.000.				
BIHUCOURT.	14·4·17	7 p.m.	No 4. Section. Work on roadway – BEUGNÂTRE – ECOUST-ST-MEIN Road at B24 d 7 8. (Sheet 57c 1/40.000).	[signature]
-do-	15·4·17	–	No 1 Section. – as on 14·4·1917. – No. 3 Section – as on 14·4·1917. " 2 " Work on roadway VRAUCOURT – ECOUST. No 4 -do- -do-	[signature]
-do-	16·4·17		No. 1 Section – as on 15·4·1917. No. 3 Section – as on 15·4·1917 – " 2 " -do- -do- No 4 -do- Standings and approaches to water troughs B26 a 1 9 (Sheet 57c 1/40.000)	[signature]
-do-	17·4·17		No 1. Section – as on 16·4·1917. No 2 Section – as on 16·4·1917. " 3 " Deviation ~~for~~ road round crater (at C8 a 2 0. Sheet 57c 1/40.000) No 4. Section as on 16·4·1917	[signature]
-do-	18·4·17		No 1 Section – as on 17·4·1917. No. 3 Section – as on 17·4·1917. " 2 " Crossings over trenches (about B28 b 3 3. Sheet 57c 1/40.000. No. 4 Section -do-	[signature]
-do-	19·4·17		No 1 Section Deviation of road round crater (at C8 a 2 0. Sheet 57c 1/40000) No 2 Section – as on 18·4·1917. " 3 " -do- -do- No 4 " -do-	[signature]
-do-	20·4·17		No. 1 Section – as on 19·4·1917. – and road repair VRAUCOURT-ECOUST Road) No 3. " as on 19·4·1917. " 2 " -do- " 4 " -do-	[signature]
-do-	21·4·17		No. 4 Section as on 20·4·1917. " 3 " as on 20·4·1917 " 2 " -do-	
		1.15	" ~~#~~ 1 " Proceeded by march route to MORY (5K 28.) and billeted – Work on VRAUCOURT – ECOUST road. Major C. Bamford evacuated to Hospital (sick)	[signature]

T2134. Wt. W708–776. 500000. 4/15. Sir J. C. & S.

Instructions regarding War Diaries and Intelligence Summaries are contained in F. S. Regs., Part II. and the Staff Manual respectively. Title pages will be prepared in manuscript.

WAR DIARY
or
~~INTELLIGENCE~~ SUMMARY.
(Erase heading not required.)

Army Form C. 2118.

Place	Date	Hour	Summary of Events and Information	Remarks and references to Appendices
Reference Map:-			LENS 11. 1/100.000	
BIHUCOURT.	22:4:17	9·30	No 4. Section proceeded by march route to MORY. (5K28) and billeted – Work on VRAUCOURT - ECOUST Road.	
			No. 1 " Work on VRAUCOURT - ECOUST road. No. 2 Section – As on 21:4:1917 –	
			No 3 " Standings and approaches to water troughs (at H8d56 Sheet 57c 1/40.000)	[signature]
do	23:4:17		No 2 Section as on 22:4:1917. No 3 Section – as on 22:4:1917 –	
MORY.	do		" 1 " as on 22:4:1917 No 4 Section – as on 22:4:1917 –	[signature]
BIHUCOURT	24:4:17		No. 2 Section. Standings and approaches to water troughs (at H8d56 Sheet 57c 1/40.000) No 3 Section – as on 23:4:1917	
MORY	do		No 1 do as on 23:4:1917. No 4. Section – as on 23:4:1917	[signature]
BIHUCOURT.	25:4:17		No: 2 Section. BIHUCOURT - VRAUCOURT overland track No 3 Section – as on 24:4:1917.	
MORY	do		No 1 " as on 24:4:1917. No 4 do – as on 24:4:1917	
	do		One sapper wounded (No 504590 Sapper Smith P.G)	[signature]
BIHUCOURT.	26:4:17		No: 2 Section – as on 25:4:1917. No 3 Section – as on 25:4:1917.	
			" 1 " do do " 4 " do do	[signature]

T2134. Wt. W708–776. 500000. 4/15. Sir J. C. & S.

Instructions regarding War Diaries and Intelligence Summaries are contained in F. S. Regs., Part II. and the Staff Manual respectively. Title pages will be prepared in manuscript.

WAR DIARY
or
~~INTELLIGENCE SUMMARY.~~
(Erase heading not required.)

Army Form C. 2118.

503rd Field Co RE

Vol 5

Place	Date	Hour	Summary of Events and Information	Remarks and references to Appendices
Reference Map:- LENS 11. 1/100.000.				
MORY.	27.4.17		No 1 Section:- Road repairs VRAUCOURT - ECOUST road. No 4. Section:- BIHUCOURT - VRAUCOURT overland track.	[signature] Capt
BIHUCOURT	do		No 2 Section:- BIHUCOURT - VRAUCOURT overland track. No. 3 Section Standings and approaches to water troughs (H 8d 56, 57c 1/40.000)	
MORY	28.4.17		No 1 Section as on 27.4.1917. No 4 Section as on 27.4.1917.	
BIHUCOURT	do		No 2 Section as on 27.4.1917. No 3 Section as on 27.4.1917.	[signature] Capt
MORY.	29.4.17		No. 1 Section as on 28.4.1917. No 4 Section as on 28.4.1917 & ACHIET-LE-GRAND MORY overland track	
BIHUCOURT.	do		No 2 Section as on 28.4.1917. No 3 Section as on 28.4.1917.	[signature] Capt
MORY	30.4.17		No 1 Section as on 29.4.1917. No 4 Section as on 29.4.1917	
BIHUCOURT.	do		No 2 Section as on 29.4.1917. No 3 Section as on 29.4.1917	[signature] Capt

T2134. Wt. W708—776. 500000. 4/15. Sir J. C. & S.

Instructions regarding War Diaries and Intelligence Summaries are contained in F. S. Regs., Part II. and the Staff Manual respectively. Title pages will be prepared in manuscript.

WAR DIARY
or
~~INTELLIGENCE SUMMARY~~.
(Erase heading not required.)

Army Form C. 2118.

503 [illegible]

Place	Date	Hour	Summary of Events and Information	Remarks and references to Appendices
Reference Map - LENS 11 1/100,000.				
MORY	1:5:17	-	No: 1 Section. Road repairs. VRAUCOURT - ECOUST road. No 4 Section { BIHUCOURT - VRAUCOURT overland track. ACHIET-LE-GRAND - MORY overland track.	
BIHUCOURT	do	-	No: 2 Section ACHIET-LE-GRAND - MORY overland track. BIHUCOURT - VRAUCOURT overland track. No 3 Section Standings and	
do	do		approaches to water troughs (H3d 56 Ref Map - Sheet 57c 1/40,000)	[signature] Capt
do	do		Reinforcement:- 2 Sappers (No.176989 Sapper Pearson J.H. No 167738 Sapper Hoult C)	
MORY	2:5:17		Nos 1 & 4 Sections. - Inspection of arms, ammunition, gas helmets &c.	
BIHUCOURT	do		Nos 2 & 3 do do do	[signature] Capt
MORY	3:5:17		Nos 1 & 4 Sections - as on 1st May 1917.	
BIHUCOURT	do		Nos 2 & 3 do do	[signature] Capt
do	do		Reinforcement:- 2 Sappers (No 438412 Sapper Warren J.J. No 3551 Sapper Surkees W.R).	
MORY	4:5:17		Nos 1 & 4 Sections - as on 3rd May 1917.	
BIHUCOURT	do		Nos 2 & 3 do do	
do	do	5:30pm	Headquarters, Nos 2 & 3 Sections proceeded by march route to VRAUCOURT and encamped near Sugar Factory	[signature]
MORY	do	6:30	Nos 1 & 4 Sections do do do do	[signature] Capt
VRAUCOURT.	5:5:17		Nos. 1. 2. 3 & 4 Sections at Works as on 4: 5: 1917.	[signature] Capt
do	6:5:17		Nos 1. 2. 3 & 4 Sections at Works as on 5: 5: 1917.	[signature] Capt

T2134. Wt. W708-776. 500000. 4/15. Sir J. C. & S.

Instructions regarding War Diaries and Intelligence Summaries are contained in F. S. Regs., Part II. and the Staff Manual respectively. Title pages will be prepared in manuscript.

WAR DIARY
or
~~INTELLIGENCE~~ SUMMARY.
(Erase heading not required.)

Army Form C. 2118.

503rd Fd Co RE

Place	Date	Hour	Summary of Events and Information	Remarks and references to Appendices
Reference Map:-			LENS 11 1/100.000	
VRAUCOURT	7.5.17		No. 1 Section. Filling in crater at C7d82 Ref Map 57c 1/40.000. No. 2 Section Overland tracks.	
do	do		No. 3 Section Filling in crater at C8a0.2 do No. 4 Section Overland tracks.	[initials] Capt
do	8.5.17		No. 1 Section:- Drill:- rifle exercises &c. Nos 2.3 & 4 Sections as on 7.5.1917	[initials] Capt
do	9.5.17		No 1 Section Filling in crater at C7d 8 2 Ref Map 57c 1/40000. No 2 Section Overland tracks. No 3 Section Filling in crater at C8 a 0.2. — " — No 4 Section — do —	SWC
			Major S.W. Chapman, from Adjutant 58th Divisional Engineers assumed Command of Coy	SWC
do	10.5.17		No 1 Section Filling in crater at C 7 d 8 2 Ref Map 57c 1/40 000 No 2 Section Overland tracks No 3 Section Filling in crater at C8 a 0.2. — " — . No 4 — " — — " —	SWC
do	11.5.17		Camp shelled, moved unit to fresh camp site at B 29 c 8 8 No 2 Section moved to camp at BIHUCOURT at G 12 c 6.5 No 1 Section filling in crater at C 7 d 8.2 No 3. Filling in crater at C 8 a 0.2. No 4, overland tracks	SWC
do	12.5.17		No 1 Section filling in crater at C 7 d 8 2. No 2 Section Overland Track ACHIET LE GRAND G.10. central to BIEFVILLERS. H 19. central Ref Map 57c 1/40 000, No 3 Section filling in crater at C 8 a 0.2 No 4 Section Overland tracks. Handed over all work in hand to OC 511th Field Co RE	SWC

T2134. Wt. W708–776. 500000. 4/15. Sir J. C. & S.

Instructions regarding War Diaries and Intelligence Summaries are contained in F. S. Regs., Part II. and the Staff Manual respectively. Title pages will be prepared in manuscript.

WAR DIARY

or

~~INTELLIGENCE SUMMARY.~~

(Erase heading not required.)

503rd Field Coy RE

Army Form C. 2118.

Place	Date	Hour	Summary of Events and Information	Remarks and references to Appendices
VRAUCOURT	13.5.17		Coy at disposal of OC for training. ~~[illegible]~~ No 508490. Private P. BIRCH - RAMC 3/1st London Field Ambulance, killed whilst on duty at water filling point at MORY, and No 504752 Driver John PERRY RE (TF) wounded 2 horses wounded, & water cart damaged. No 2 Section returned from BIHUCOURT	SMC
– " –	14.5.17		Coy training, ~~[illegible]~~ 2 wounded horses removed to Mobile Vety Section	SMC
– " –	15.5.17		Coy training, OC ~~[illegible]~~ went round works being carried out by OC 95th Field Co RE in B 17 + 18. Ref Map Sheet 57c NW. No 8869 Sapr BLOOMFIELD W, " [illegible] " [illegible] N, reinforcements for No 6 Gen[illegible]	SMC
"	16.5.17		Coy Training. 2 Sections carry out training on Reserve line, + [illegible] work completed. 50x wiring, + 40x trench + 1 machine gun emplacement made	[illegible] by OC SMC
	17.5.17		Coy Training. 2 Sections on reserve line, 50x wiring completed + 50x trench deepened + provided with fire step. No 101172 CLARKE J, " 84373 " CROW H, joined from No 4 Reinforcement Coy	SMC
	18.5.17		Coy Training. 2 Sections on reserve line 150x [illegible] completed + 60x yds new trench dug. 40 yds deepened + provided with fire step	SMC
	19.5.17		Coy Training. Capt Chasey proceeded on 10 days leave of absence	SMC

T2134. Wt. W708—776. 500000. 4/15. Sir J. C. & S.

Instructions regarding War Diaries and Intelligence Summaries are contained in F. S. Regs., Part II. and the Staff Manual respectively. Title pages will be prepared in manuscript.

WAR DIARY
or
~~INTELLIGENCE SUMMARY.~~
(Erase heading not required.)

Army Form C. 2118.

503rd Fd Coy RE

Place	Date	Hour	Summary of Events and Information	Remarks and references to Appendices
VRAUCOURT	20.5.17		Coy Training	
	21.5.17		Inspection of Coy by CRE, Lt Col E M NEWELL DSO RE. Unit congratulated on turn out. No 2 (Lt COLLINS) Section + No 4 (2Lt MILLER) Section paraded at 7.45 pm for night work on communication trench at U 28.b 2, but unable to work owing to intense shell fire. 2Lt + S. MILLER, No 504569 Sgt FRANKLIN. D, wounded & evacuated to CCS. No 504318 2 Cpl SMITH. H wounded, & remained at duty.	SMC
—"—	22.5.17		3 Sappers. No 504486 ROUSELL. A No 504514 LOVELL HA + No 506539 SUTTON FG report to OC 504th Fd Coy RE for special work with R.F.A. No 2 + 4 Section (Lt COLLINS + 2Lt WOOLSTON SMITH) for night work on new C.T at U 28 b 2. accompanied by OC Coy + 2Lt BANKS. 11 L.D horses + 2 riding horses arrived for Coy. 230x C.T. dug to depth of 2', + support line taped out.	SMC
—"—	23.5.17		No I Section (Lt CHILTON) + No 3 Section (2Lt BANKS) paraded for night work on roads in ECOUST – to BULLECOURT those roads in C 2 a. b c.d. ~~+ U 27~~ C 3 a, + U 27 c+d. No 2 (Lt COLLINS) + 4 Section 2Lt WOOLSTON SMITH on forward C.T. No 504601 Driver ARTHUR. W.J. and No 504477 Dr WATSON. J.M. ~~&~~ killed whilst returning from watering parade also 5 horses killed + 2 wounded. 2 drivers joined as reinforcements No 85618 Dr SPILLING A + No 35241 Dr WILLIAMS T from No 1 Wing RE Base Depot. No 504610 Dr EDMUNDS. D.L wounded, & remained at duty.	SMC

T2134. Wt. W708–776. 500000. 4/15. Sir J. C. & S.

Instructions regarding War Diaries and Intelligence Summaries are contained in F. S. Regs., Part II. and the Staff Manual respectively. Title pages will be prepared in manuscript.

WAR DIARY
or
~~INTELLIGENCE~~ SUMMARY.
(*Erase heading not required.*)

Army Form C. 2118.

503rd Field Coy RE

Hour, Date, Place	Summary of Events and Information	Remarks and references to Appendices
VRAUCOURT. 24.5.17	No I Section. Lt CHILTON ~~night~~ and No 3 Section "Lt BANKS on Communication trench at U 28 b 2. No 2 Section Lt COLLINS + No 4 Section "Lt WOOLSTON, SMITH night work on road ECOUST – BULLECOURT. C 2 a b c d, C 3 a. + U 27 c + d. Lt CHILTON to lay out new CT from U 28 d 2 9 to U 28 d 4. 0 (approx). No 504578 Sap. GODWIN. A H wounded and evacuated to C.C.S.	SWC
– " – 25.5.17	Sections on work as for 24.5.17 + in addition No 3 Section to dig a CT from U 28 d 3. 8 to U 28 d 4. 0.	SWC
– " – "	250x dug + support line cut through to BULLECOURT AVENUE. Road ECOUST – BULLECOURT cleared of shell holes filled + road made passable for Horse Transport to the railway embankment at U 27 d 15.55	SWC

S W Chapman Major
OC 503rd Fd Co RE

(73989) W4141—463. 400,000. 9/14. H.&J.Ltd. Forms/C. 2118/10.

Ref Map Sheet 51B. SW 1/20,000

Instructions regarding War Diaries and Intelligence Summaries are contained in F. S. Regs., Part II. and the Staff Manual respectively. Title pages will be prepared in manuscript.

WAR DIARY
or
INTELLIGENCE ~~SUMMARY~~.
(*Erase heading not required.*)

Army Form C. 2118.

503rd Field Coy RE

Hour, Date, Place	Summary of Events and Information	Remarks and references to Appendices
26.5.17. VRAUCOURT	No 1. 3 & 4 Sections under Lt BANKS work on CT from U 28 d 3-8 to U 28 d 4. 0. 250x dug to average depth of 2'	SMC
	No 2 Section resting. Road reconnaissance at U 27 d 1.4 to U 27.d 7.0 on to C 2 c 3 2 by Lt CHILTON (57c NE 1/40,000)	
27.5.17 —"—	No 2 Section making fascines. No 1 3 & 4 resting. No 504251 Dr Perry went to V Corps rest camp at ST VALERY SUR SOMME	SMC
	No 2 —"— work on crater in ECOUST by night	
28.5.17	No 1 & 3 Sections fitting & packing Elephant Shelter ready for transport to the line. No 2 & 4 Section making fascines. Handed over work on C.T. to 24th Bn Manchester (Pioneers) on night of 27/28. May.	This work from 8 am to 1 pm. Sections to be ready to go on night work if required. SMC
29.5.17 "	No 1 Section & 3 Section on Crater in ECOUST. No 4 Section fixing water tanks at U 27 d 3.5. No 2 Section fixing shelter in Ry Bank at C 5 a 2.3. No 504443 Sap TARGETT J. wounded and evacuated to Hospital No 504326 L/Cpl BISHOP P.A. No 504420 Sap JONES L.V. slightly wounded & remained at duty. Two drivers No 504320 Dr HILLIER J. and No 508050 Dr BOYLES joined as reinforcements from No 2 Wing RE Base Depot	SMC
30.5.17	All sections resting.	
31.5.17	No 1 section in camp No 2. 3 & 4 Section on road repair in MORY. 1 NCO & 2 men with Infantry party on repair ST LEGER road. No 183684 Sap FIELDER W.H. joined as reinforcement from No 3 Reinforcement Coy RE	SMC

S H Chapman Maj
RE 503 Fd Coy RE

(73989) W4141—463. 400,000. 9/14. H.&J.Ltd. Forms/C. 2118/10.

Instructions regarding War Diaries and Intelligence Summaries are contained in F. S. Regs., Part II. and the Staff Manual respectively. Title pages will be prepared in manuscript.

WAR DIARY
or
INTELLIGENCE SUMMARY.
(Erase heading not required.)

Army Form C. 2118.

503rd Field Coy RE

Vol 6

Hour, Date, Place		Summary of Events and Information	Remarks and references to Appendices
1-6-17.	VRAUCOURT.	No 1 & 4 Sections working on roads and craters in and round MORY. No 2 Section in Camp. No 3 section on P of W. Cage MORY. 1 NCO and 2 Spr & Infantry party on repair of MORY - St LEGER road. Major Chapman proceeded on 10 days leave of absence. 476023 Spr Middleton W. 127081 Spr Ward H. 34313 Dr Blades W. 80784 Dr Brown A. & 61027 Dr Tigg G. joined as reinforcements from No 6 Re-inforcement Camp.	[initials]
2-6-17	"	No 1, 2 & 4 Sections on roads & craters in & round MORY. No 3 section in Camp. 1 NCO & 2 Spr with Infantry party on repair of MORY - St LEGER road. 8 p.m. Company moved Camp to MORY. B.21.c.3.7.	[initials]
3-6-17	MORY.	No 1 & 3 Sections on roads & craters in and round MORY. No 2 section on A.S.C. road MORY. No 4 section in Camp. 1 NCO & 2 Spr with Infantry party on repair of MORY - St LEGER road. Capt Chasey reported from leave	[initials]
4.6.17	-do-	Nos 1 & 3 Sections in camp. No 2 Section on A.S.C road MORY - No 4 Section repairing MORY - ECOUST road.	[signature]
5.6.17	-do-	No 1 Section erecting shelters in trench at U22c52 - Widening & deepening communication trench U27b53 to U27b88. No 2 Section - widening and deepening RAILWAY TRENCH No. 3 Section. Wire entanglement. RAILWAY TRENCH - No 4 Section - Widening and deepening BULLECOURT AVENUE.	[signature]
6.6.1917	-do-	No 1 Section. Deepening trench from U28a53 to U28a88. Excavating C.T. from U27b53 to U27b88. - No 2 Section excavating ~~trench~~ for elephant shelters in RAILWAY TRENCH. - No 3 Section wire entanglements RAILWAY TRENCH. No 4 Section. Widening and deepening C.T. BULLECOURT AVENUE.	[signature]
7.6.1917	-do-	No 1 Section Excavating trench from U28a53 to U28a88. Erecting shelter at U22c52 Excavating C.T. from U27b53 to U27b88. No 2 Section Excavating for elephant shelters in RAILWAY TRENCH No 3 Section. erecting wire entanglements RAILWAY TRENCH. No 4 Section Widening and deepening BULLECOURT AVENUE. No 504321 2nd Corpl PALMER E.G. slightly wounded and remained on duty.	[signature]

(73989) W4141—463. 400,000. 9/14. H.&J.Ltd. Forms/C. 2118/10.

Instructions regarding War Diaries and Intelligence Summaries are contained in F. S. Regs., Part II. and the Staff Manual respectively. Title pages will be prepared in manuscript.

WAR DIARY
or
~~INTELLIGENCE SUMMARY.~~ 503rd FIELD COMPANY ROYAL ENGINEERS.

(*Erase heading not required.*)

Army Form C. 2118.

Hour, Date, Place		Summary of Events and Information	Remarks and references to Appendices
Reference Map: Trench Map ECOUST-ST-MEIN 1/10,000.			
8:6:1917	MORY.	No. 1 Section. Widening and deepening RAILWAY TRENCH. – No 2 Section – erecting Elephant Shelters RAILWAY TRENCH. No 3 Section Widening and deepening RAILWAY TRENCH. No 4 Section erecting elephant shelters RAILWAY TRENCH.	[signature] Capt
9:6:1917	-do-	No. 1 Section, erecting O.P. at U28a42. – No 2 Section, wire entanglements RAILWAY TRENCH. – No 3 Section – Widening and deepening RAILWAY TRENCH & constructing elephant shelter. No 4 Section Excavating C.T. from U27b53 to U27b88. Fixing elephant shelters at U22c81.	[signature] Capt
10.6.1917	-do-	No 1 Section Preparing wooden shelters R.E. Dump MORY. – No 2 Section wire entanglements RAILWAY TRENCH. No 3. Section. Excavating RAILWAY TRENCH. No 4 Section Completing L.Gun position at U28a88. Excavating C.T. U28a53 to U28a88. II Lieut J.H.W. SMITH and 11 Sapper proceeded to Rest Camp. No 504351 Corpl BULL reported from No 2 wing R.E. Base as reinforcement.	[signature] Capt
11.6.1917	-do-	No 1 Section, Widening & deepening BULLECOURT AVENUE. Preparing wooden shelters at R.E. Dump MORY. – No 2 Wire entanglement RAILWAY TRENCH. – No 3 Section – Widening trench – constructing firebays & shelters RAILWAY TRENCH. – No 4 Section erecting shelters in trench U22c52 approx.	[signature] Capt
12:6:1917	-do-	No. 1 Section Widening & deepening BULLECOURT AVENUE. No 2 Section Wire entanglement in front of RAILWAY TRENCH and digging RAILWAY TRENCH. – No 3 Section Constructing firebays and shelters RAILWAY TRENCH. No 4 Section erecting shelters in trench U22c52 approx.	[signature] Capt
13.6.1917	-do-	No. 1 Section. Widening & deepening BULLECOURT AVENUE – No 2 Section Wire entanglement RAILWAY TRENCH. – No 3 Section Constructing firebays & erecting shelters RAILWAY TRENCH. No 4 Section. Digging RAILWAY TRENCH from U27d05 to U27c6075. Major S.W. Chapman returned from leave to England.	[signature] Capt
14.6.17	-do-	No 1 Section Widening & deepening BULLECOURT AVENUE. No 2 Section Wire Entanglements RAILWAY TRENCH. No 3 Section Constructing firebays & shelters in RAILWAY TRENCH. No 4 Section Digging RAILWAY TRENCH from U27d05 to U27c60.75.	[signature] Maj

Instructions regarding War Diaries and Intelligence Summaries are contained in F. S. Regs., Part II. and the Staff Manual respectively. Title pages will be prepared in manuscript.

WAR DIARY
or
~~INTELLIGENCE SUMMARY.~~

(*Erase heading not required.*)

Army Form C. 2118.

503rd (Wx) Fd Co RE

Ref ~~Trench Map~~ ECOUST-ST MEIN 1/10000

Hour, Date, Place	Summary of Events and Information	Remarks and references to Appendices
15.6.17 MORY	No 1 Section widening & deepening BULLECOURT AVENUE. No 2 Section wire entanglement RAILWAY TRENCH. No 3 Section constructing fire bays ~~shelter~~ in RAILWAY TRENCH. No 4 Section, digging RAILWAY TRENCH from U 27 d 05 to U 27 c 6075	SMC Maj
16.6.17 -do-	Handed over work to 511th Field Coy RE. Work on MORY ECOUST road on maintenance of road. Capt CHASEY & 18 OR work on GORDON SWITCH deepening & widening. Lt CHILTON & 12 OR deepening & widening front line trench	SMC Maj
17.6.17 -do-	MAINTENANCE of MORY-ECOUST road. Repair to water troughs at ST LEGER & fencing off water point. Section drill. Inspection of arms, clothing, equipment, gas mask & respirator & iron rations. Lt BANKS proceeded on leave to ENGLAND	SMC Maj
18.6.17 -do-	Maintenance of MORY ECOUST road. Lt CHILTON & 40 O.R. digging C.T. at U 27 b 1.6 to U 27 b 2.8. No 554123 Sap HEADONS reported as reinforcement from No 3 Reinforcement Coy RE. No 504374 Sap STEER. P.H. wounded	SMC Maj
19.6.17 -do-	Maintenance of MORY-ECOUST road, erecting camouflage on SUCERIE-ECOUST road. Improving Coy HQ at U 21 c 55.05 clearing culvert at U 26 c 7.1	SMC Maj
20.6.17 do	Maintenance of MORY-ECOUST road, erecting camouflage on SUCERIE-ECOUST road	SMC Maj
21.6.17 do	As for 20th June.	SMC Maj
22.6.17 do	As for 20th June.	SMC Maj
23.6.17 do	No 1-3 & 4 Sections dismantling camp, packing vehicles etc. No 2 Section moved to camp at G 2 c 3.7 (Ref Map 57C 1/40000)	SMC Maj
24.6.17 do	Unit moved to camp at G 2 c 3.7 (Ref Map 57C 1/40000)	SMC Maj

Instructions regarding War Diaries and Intelligence Summaries are contained in F. S. Regs., Part II. and the Staff Manual respectively. Title pages will be prepared in manuscript.

WAR DIARY
or
~~INTELLIGENCE~~ SUMMARY.
(Erase heading not required.)

Army Form C. 2118.

503rd Field Coy RE

Hour, Date, Place	Summary of Events and Information	Remarks and references to Appendices
25 6 17 LOGEAST WOOD (57c G 2 c 3 7).	All Sections collecting stores for Infantry Officers & NCOs class. No 99309 Sap PAGET S & No 438194 Spr JONES H reported as reinforcement from No 2 Reinforcement Coy RE	SWC Maj
26. 6 17 — " —	Capt CHASEY & Lt CHILTON with 3 NCOs & 6 Sappers per Section instructing officers & NCOs from each Battalion of 175th Inf Bde in Military Engineering. No 1, 2 & 4 Sections collecting stores, No 3 Section resting. No 506539 Sap SUTTON S No 504514 Sap LOVELL HA & No 504309 Sap ROUSELL J.R. reported from 511th Fd CoRE after work with RFA.	SWC Maj
~~27 6 17~~ "		
27-6-17 "	No 1. 3 & 4 Section work in camp. No 2 Section detailed for work on reserve line L'HOMME-MORT – ST. LEGER. Section moved to billet at ST LEGER at B4 a 2 8 under 2Lt COLLINS. (Ref Map 57C NW 1/20000)	SWC Maj
28. 6 17 "	No 1. 3 & 4 Section work in Camp No 2 Section work on reserve line L'HOMME-MORT – ST LEGER.	SWC Maj
29. 6 17 "	No 1. 3 & 4 Section in camp. No 2 Section reserve line L'HOMME-MORT – ST LEGER. Lt BARRS returned from leave to ENGLAND	SWC Maj
30. 6 17	No 1 & 4 Sections in Camp. No 3 Section under Lt BARRS relieved No 2 Section & took over billets and work at ST LEGER. No 2 Section under Lt COLLINS rejoined Coy. 2Lt EAJ BILHAM joined for duty from ROUEN	SWC Maj

S W Chapman Major
OC 503rd Field CoRE

(73989) W4141—463. 400,000. 9/14. H.&J.Ltd. Forms/C. 2118/10.

Vol 7

Army Form C. 2118.

WAR DIARY
or
~~INTELLIGENCE SUMMARY.~~

503rd Field Co RE

(*Erase heading not required.*)

Instructions regarding War Diaries and Intelligence Summaries are contained in F. S. Regs., Part II. and the Staff Manual respectively. Title pages will be prepared in manuscript.

Hour, Date, Place	Summary of Events and Information	Remarks and references to Appendices
Ref Map 57C.		
LOGEAT WOOD (Q.2 c 3.7) 1.7.17	No 3 Section "Lt BANKS T relieved No 2 Section Lt COLLINS at St LEGER (B 4 a 2 8) & No 2 Section rejoined Coy HQ Remainder of Coy resting	SM May
– do – 2.7.17	Coy resting. Lt COLLINS proceeded on leave to ENGLAND Received 175th Infantry Brigade Warning Order to move	SM May
– do – 3.7.17	Lt CHILTON & 2Lt WOOLSTON SMITH & 6 O Rank proceeded to HAVRINCOURT WOOD (Ref Map 57C) to take over work from 429th Field Coy & 427 Fd Co RE respectively Coy prepared to move	SM
– do – 4.7.17 / – do – 5.7.17	No 90048 Sap EVANS. W reported as reinforcement from No 5 Reinforcement Coy RE. Unit Marched to BANCOURT Bivouacked for the night	SM
BANCOURT. 6.7.17 (H 36 central)	Unit marched to YTRES O 20 d & bivouacked for night	SM
YTRES. 7.7.17 O 20 d	Unit marched to HAVRINCOURT WOOD & took over camp from & work of 429th Field CoRE. No 504458 Sap BENCE. W transferred to I Army School of Instruction	SM. Transport at YTRES SM
HAVRINCOURT WOOD (P 18 central) 8.7.17	Took over work of 427th Field Coy RE. Nos 2 & 4 Sections moved to camp at Q 8 O.5. Work of Coy on trench system extends from Q 5 a 0.0 to CANAL DU NORD. Q 32 a 8.9. No 1 Section work on outpost line & [illegible] line (shelters) from Q 5 a 0.0 to Q No 2 Sect from Q to Q	SM – do –
– " – 9.7.17	No 3 Section work on outpost & [illegible] line from Q to Q & No 4 Section from Q to Q	SM – do –

(73989) W4141—463. 400,000. 9/14. H.&J.Ltd. Forms/C. 2118/10.

Army Form C. 2118.

Instructions regarding War Diaries and Intelligence Summaries are contained in F. S. Regs., Part II. and the Staff Manual respectively. Title pages will be prepared in manuscript.

WAR DIARY
or
~~INTELLIGENCE SUMMARY.~~ 503rd 2nd Co RE

(Erase heading not required.)

Hour, Date, Place	Summary of Events and Information	Remarks and references to Appendices
Ref Map 57.C Edition 2		
HAVRINCOURT WOOD 10.7.17	Work on front line trenches. No 1 Section shelters No 2 Section Communication trench TUFNELL AVENUE from Q3 D 04 to Q3d 03 + drainage of front line trench No 3 + 4 Section shelters	Transport at YTRES. O.20.d SMC
—"— 11.7.17	Work as detailed for 10th inst. No 554123 Sapper MEADOWS transferred to 511th (London) Field Coy and No 504636 Sap CALLARD. 504452 Sap MAGGS. No 504040 Sap WINCKWORTH attached to 511th (London) Field Coy to act as Instructors to RAA Pioneers. No 504431 L/Cpl WHITTAKER. W.E. wounded evacuated to CCS	SM
—"— 12.7.17	Work on front line trenches continued. Shelters + communication trenches	SM
" 13.7.17	Work on front line trenches continued	SM
14.7.17	Work on front line trenches continued. Lt FG COLLINS returned from leave to United Kingdom	SM SM
—"— 15.7.17	Work on front line trenches continued. Lt CC CUNNINGHAM reported for duty. 2/Lt E. MARR reported for duty from RE Base ROUEN.	SM
—"— 16.7.17	Work on front line trenches continued. Coy HQ moved to RUYAULCOURT. P10.C.3.9.	SM
RUYAULCOURT 17.7.17	Work on front line trenches continued. No 504503. Sap SAUNDERS L killed + No 504089 Sap COLLINS F wounded	SM
18.7.17	Work on front line trenches.	SM
19.7.17	Work on front line trenches. No 2 Section joined Coy HQ at RUYAULCOURT	SM

(73989) W4141—463. 400,000. 9/14. H.&J.Ltd. Forms/C. 2118/10.

Instructions regarding War Diaries and Intelligence Summaries are contained in F. S. Regs., Part II. and the Staff Manual respectively. Title pages will be prepared in manuscript.

WAR DIARY

or

~~INTELLIGENCE SUMMARY.~~

(Erase heading not required.)

Army Form C. 2118.

503rd Field Coy RE

Hour, Date, Place	Summary of Events and Information	Remarks and references to Appendices
Ref Map 57.c 1/20.000		
RUYALCOURT 20. 7. 17	No 1. 2 & 4 Section work on front line trenches. No 3 Sect work in Camp & Divisional Bath at RUYALCOURT	SM
" 21. 7. 17	No 1. 2 & 4 Section work in front line trenches. No 3 Section work on Divisional Bath at RUYALCOURT	SM
" 22. 7. 17	Detail of work for Sections as for 21st inst. No 459691 Sapr SUTTON and No 504512 Sapr HARDICK took part in raid by 2/9 London Regt.	SM
" 23. 7. 17	Detail of work for Sections as for 21st inst. 175 Inf Bde Warning order for move received.	SM
" 24. 7. 17	No 459691 Sapr SUTTON ~~wounded~~ & L/Cpl CUNNINGHAM posted to 504th Fd Coy RE to date from 22.7.17. Detail of work for Sections as for 21st	SM
" 25. 7. 17	Detail of work of Sections as for 21st. Lt BARTLETT. A.L. reported for duty from 508th [illegible] Fd Coy RE. Handing over works, documents &c to OC 64th Field Coy RE and accompanied him round the trench system & back area.	SM
" 26. 7. 17	No 1. 2 & 4 Section rejoined Coy HQ at RUYALCOURT on completion of relief by 64th Fd Coy RE. Transport & mounted portion proceeded by march route to ABLAINZEVILLE (LENS 11 [illegible] 8.8).	SM
27. 7. 17	Dismounted portion of Coy paraded at 4 am & marched to [illegible] Light railway [illegible] & entrained for [illegible] [illegible] detrained & boarded train with [illegible] [illegible] of Infantry of 175 Bde & entrained at 12 noon for SAULTY (LENS 11 R.3 a.6.5) detrained at 4 pm & unloaded train. On completion marched to camp at FOSSEUX (LENS 11 [illegible]). MOUNTED portion moved from ABLAINZEVILLE	SM

(73989) W4141—463. 400,000. 9/14. H.&J.Ltd. Forms/C. 2118/10.

Instructions regarding War Diaries and Intelligence Summaries are contained in F. S. Regs., Part II. and the Staff Manual respectively. Title pages will be prepared in manuscript.

WAR DIARY
or
~~INTELLIGENCE SUMMARY~~. 503rd Field Coy RE

(*Erase heading not required.*)

Army Form C. 2118.

Hour, Date, Place	Summary of Events and Information	Remarks and references to Appendices
~~Ref Map 57c 1/20000~~ ~~HAVRINCOURT P10C3.9~~ FOSSEUX LENS 11 G 3.8.1. 28.7.17	Coy settling in camp. Overhauling Vehicles, tools clothing + equipment. Brigadier General Commanding 175th Infantry Bde congratulated OC Coy on the good work performed by the unit at HAVRINCOURT and expressed ~~his~~ appreciation. OC Coy visited CRE 12th Division with reference to work to be done by 503rd Field Coy REs under his orders.	SWC
" 29.7.17	Dismounted portion prepared to move.	SWC
" 30.7.17	Dismounted portion moved by bus from FOSSEUX to bivouac at H 32 C 5 3. (Sheet 51b)	
H 32 C 5 3. (Sheet 51 b) 31.7.17	OC + Section Officers reconnoitred work to be done on EAST RESERVE trench. MONCHY (O 1 b 4 4). Sections improving bivouac. All sections paraded at 8.45 pm for work on trench as above.	SWC

S. W. Chapman Major
OC 503 Fd Co REs

(73989) W4141—463. 400,000. 9/14. H.&J.Ltd. Forms/C. 2118/10.

Instructions regarding War Diaries and Intelligence Summaries are contained in F. S. Regs., Part II. and the Staff Manual respectively. Title pages will be prepared in manuscript.

WAR DIARY
or
~~INTELLIGENCE~~ SUMMARY.
(*Erase heading not required.*)

Army Form C. 2118.

503rd Field Coy R.E.

Hour, Date, Place		Summary of Events and Information	Remarks and references to Appendices
Ref Map 51 b			
H32.c.5.3	1.8.17	All sections on night work on EAST RESERVE TRENCH MONCHY (O1 + 4.4)	Transport at FOSSEUX LENS 11 S.3 E.1 SM
-"-	2.8.17	Working parties returned from trenches on account of raid & barrage by Enemy which made work impossible	SML
-"-	3.8.17	2 Sections (No 2 + 3) work in Camp. No 1 + 4 for work in trenches at night	SM
-"-	4.8.17	No 1 + 4 Sections night work in trenches, No 2 + 3 day work fixing A frames & widening trench	SM
-"-	5.8.17	No 1 + 4 Sections night work, deepening & widening trench	
		No 2 + 3 Section day work fixing "A frames & ragging	SM
-"-		Following Sappers reported from No 3 Reinforcement Coy RE & are taken on strength of Coy from 31.7.17	
		No 478586 Sap EARNSHAW J. 97790 ALDRIDGE J. 496978 SILVO H.A.J 184401 PARSONS W.R 23609 LINDOP S.J.	SM
		No 459691 Sap SURTEES W reported from C.C.S. for duty	SM
-"-	6.8.17	No 1 + 4 Section day work in trenches, widening & deepening trench & fixing "A" frames No 2 + 3 night work deepening trench	SM

Army Form C. 2118.

WAR DIARY
or
INTELLIGENCE SUMMARY.

(Erase heading not required.)

503rd Field Coy RE

Instructions regarding War Diaries and Intelligence Summaries are contained in F. S. Regs., Part II. and the Staff Manual respectively. Title pages will be prepared in manuscript.

Hour, Date, Place		Summary of Events and Information	Remarks and references to Appendices
Ref Map 51.b			
H32.c.5.3.	7.8.17	No work in trenches by day owing to preparation for operations. Nos 2 + 3 Section work in EAST RESERVE at night. Following Sappers reported as reinforcement from No 4 Reinforcement Coy RE & are taken on strength of Coy from 6.8.17. No 495039. B CARTER. No 498519. R A COOPER	SM
-"-	8.8.17.	No work in trenches by day. No 2+3 Section work on EAST RESERVE by night. No 504404 Driver BROOM reported for duty from ROUEN.	SM
-"-	9.8.17	No work in trenches owing to operations. Inspection of Clothing, Equipt. Arms Ammunition of each Section	SM SM
-"-	10.8.17	No 2+3 Section work in trenches by day No 1+4 by night	SM
-"-	11.8.17	No 2+3 Section work in trenches by day No 1+4 by night	SM
-"-	12.8.17	No 2+3 Section work in trenches by day No work at night	SM
-"-	13.8.17	No 1+4 Section work in trenches by day Nos 2+3 Section by night	SM
-"-	14.8.17	No 1+4 Section work in trenches by day, No 2+3 Section by night. *No 1752 Dr COOPER F reported from RE Base Depot as reinforcement & taken on strength as from 13th-8-17. No 183684 Sap FIELDER H slightly wounded remained at duty	SM SM *Previous unit 1/2 H.C. 3rd Coy RE

Instructions regarding War Diaries and Intelligence Summaries are contained in F. S. Regs., Part II. and the Staff Manual respectively. Title pages will be prepared in manuscript.

WAR DIARY
or
~~INTELLIGENCE SUMMARY~~. 503rd Fd Coy R.E.

(*Erase heading not required.*)

Army Form C. 2118.

Hour, Date, Place	Summary of Events and Information	Remarks and references to Appendices
Ref Map 51b H32 C 5 3. 15 8 17	No 1 + 4 Section work in trenches by day No 2 + 3 work by night. No 556393 Spr MAC DIARMID reported as reinforcement from No 5 Reinforcement Coy RE	SM
— " — 16 8 17	No work by day. No 1 + 4 Sections work in trenches by night	SM
— " — 17 8 17	No 2 + 3 Section at work in trenches by day No 1 + 4 by night	SM Lt CHILTON [illegible] to ENGLAND
— " — 18 8 17	No 2 + 3 Section at work in trenches by day No 1 + 4 by night	SM
— " — 19 8 17	No 2 + 3 Section at work in trenches by day No work at night	SM
" 20 8 17	Unit moved to DUISANS (L 7 a 9.0 Sheet 51c 1/40000)	SM
DUISANS L7.a.9.0, 51.c 1/40000 21 8 17	Mounted portion marched from FOSSEUX & rejoin unit at DUISSANS	SM
22 8 17	Inspection of Transport by A.A. + Q.M.G. 58th Division Received letter of thanks for work done by Coy at Monchy & congratulations of CRE on skill shown by unit in carrying out work in a very exposed position without being discovered by the enemy	SM
	2Lt BARTLETT posted to 504th Fd Coy RE under orders of CRE	SM
— " — 23 8 17	Painting Vehicles, overhauling clothing & equipment	SM
— " — 24 8 17	Packing Vehicles ready for move	SM
— " — 25 8 17	Unit marched to ARRAS & entrained for PROVEN (Ref Map HAZEBROUCK 1/100000 ~~Sheet~~ H.2.9.7) & detrained & marched to camp at G6 a 5.8 (Ref Map Sheet 28)	SM

(73989) W4141—463. 400,000. 9/14. H.&J.Ltd. Forms/C. 2118/10.

Instructions regarding War Diaries and Intelligence Summaries are contained in F. S. Regs., Part II. and the Staff Manual respectively. Title pages will be prepared in manuscript.

WAR DIARY
or
~~INTELLIGENCE SUMMARY.~~ 503rd Field Coy RE
(*Erase heading not required.*)

Army Form C. 2118.

Hour, Date, Place	Summary of Events and Information	Remarks and references to Appendices
Ref Map Sheet 28. N.W.		
G6.a.5.8. 26.8.17	Coy Training; 2/Lt BILHAM. E. proceeded to XVIII Corps Infantry Training School at VOLKERINCKHOVE for a course of Infantry Training	SM
—"— 27.8.17	Coy Training	SM
—"— 28.8.17	Packing Vehicles for move	SM
—"— 29.8.17	Unit marched to billets in dugout at C 25 d 3.5. & took over plan & work in hand of 475th Fd Coy RE Transport moved to H3 b 3.7 under Capt Chasey RE	SM
C 25. d 3.5. -	No. 458064 Dr BROUGH. G.A transferred from HQ 58 Div Engineers to date 24.8.17 Lt CHILTON returned from leave to Ud Kingdom No. 504044 Sapper HOLBROOK. H.L reported from No 3 Reinforcement Coy & taken on strength of Coy from 28.8.17	SM
—"— 30.8.17	No 1 Section cleaning Camp No 2 improving accommodation. No 3 Section repairing duckboard track & laying new one from WILSONS FARM. C26 b 4.0. to CROSS ROADS FARM at C22.c 6.8. No 4 Shelters at Advance Dressing Station	SM
—"— 31.8.17	No 1 Section repairing 2A bridge across YSER CANAL C25 central No 2 improving accommodation. No 3 duckboard tracks No 4 Shelters at A.D.S	SM

S W Chapman Maj
OC 503 Fd Co RE

(73989) W4141—463. 400,000. 9/14. H.&J.Ltd. Forms/C. 2118/10.

Instructions regarding War Diaries and Intelligence Summaries are contained in F. S. Regs., Part II. and the Staff Manual respectively. Title pages will be prepared in manuscript.

WAR DIARY
or
~~INTELLIGENCE SUMMARY.~~
(Erase heading not required.)

Army Form C. 2118.

503rd Field Coy RE

Vol 9

Ref Map Sheet 28 NW 1/20000

Hour, Date, Place		Summary of Events and Information	Remarks and references to Appendices
C 25. d 3.5.	1-9.17	No I Section, repairing bridge, + pathway on the Bank of Canal No 2 Section repairing blown in Shelter No 3 Section duckboard tracks No 4 Advanced Dressing Station	SM
"	2.9.17	No I Section repairing shelter No 2 Section repairing shelter No 3 duckboard tracks No 4 Advanced Dressing Station	SM
-"-	3.9.17	Sections employed as on 2nd inst	SM
-"-	4.9.17	-Do- -Do- -Do-	SM
-"-	5.9.17	No 2 Section proceeded to Divnl Workshops at A22 d 9.5. No 1 Section accommodation & Soup Kitchen at HILLTOP FARM C 21 d 1.8. No 3 Section Built board track No 4 Section Advanced Dressing Station	SM
-"-	6.9.17	No 1 Section Accommodation Soup Kitchen & Divisional Baths at REIGERSBURG CAMP H6 a 5.1 No 3 Section duckboard track, No 4 A D S.	SM
-"-	7.9.17	Sections employed as for 6th inst	SM
-"-	8.9.17	Nos 1 & 3 Section work as for 6th inst No 4 Section ADS & preparation of horse standings for 2 Batteries & 1 Supply Coy ASC at C 26 a 5.1	SM
-"-	9.9.17	Work as for 8th inst	SM
	10.9.17	Work as for 8th inst No 4 Section marking out site for horse standing for 2 Bdes RFA at H5 d. NO 504571 Cpl WARD. R J slightly wounded remained on duty	SM

(73989) W4141—463. 400,000. 9/14. H.&J.Ltd. Forms/C. 2118/10.

Instructions regarding War Diaries and Intelligence Summaries are contained in F. S. Regs., Part II. and the Staff Manual respectively. Title pages will be prepared in manuscript.

WAR DIARY
or
~~INTELLIGENCE~~ SUMMARY.
(Erase heading not required.)

Army Form C. 2118.

503rd Field Co RE

Hour, Date, Place		Summary of Events and Information	Remarks and references to Appendices
Reference Map Sheet 28. NW 1/20,000			
C 25 d 3.5	11.9.17	No 1 Section accommodation in Canal Bank Soup Kitchen at HILLTOP C 21 d 1.9. No 3 Section duckboard track. No 4 Section Shelter at Advanced Dressing Station Horse Standings at NOORDHOF FARM C 25 a 5.2. No 2 Section returned from Divisional Workshops. No 504523 Sap FUDJE. J.E wounded and evacuated to C.C.S. No 213609 Sap LINDOP. S.J died of wounds No 504571 Cpl WARD. R.J. slightly wounded remained at duty	SM
"	12.9.17	No 1 Section work on Soup Kitchen at HILLTOP. No 2 Section accommodation No 3 duckboard track. No 4 Horse Standings. No 90048 Sapr EVANS. W. gassed [illegible] and evacuated to CCS.	SM
	13.9.17	Work of Sections as for 12th inst	SM
	14.9.17	Work of Sections as for 12th inst. No 504324 Dr S PREADBURY S wounded & admitted to CCS	SM
	15.9.17	No 1 Section Soup Kitchen No 2 Section accommodation and clearing obstacles from bed of river STEENBEEK between ST JULIAN BRIDGE C 12 c 2 2 to bridge at C [illegible] d 1.0. No 3 Section repair of ST JULIAN BRIDGE & clearing bed of STEENBEEK from ST JULIAN to C 18 a 3.7. No 4 Horse Standings	SM
	16.9.17	Work as for 15th inst	
	17.9.17	No 1 Section Soup Kitchen No 2 Accommodation No 3 Duckboard track. ~~No~~ repairs to ST JULIAN BRIDGE No 4 Horse Standings	SM
	18.9.17	No 1 Section Soup Kitchen No 2 Accommodation No 3 Duckboard track. No 4 Resting	
	19.9.17	Coy moved into trenches at C 22 b 7.0. No ~~[illegible]~~ 2 & 3 Sect placed 32 bridges across river STEENBEEK between REGINA CROSS BRIDGE C 5 d 05.05 & ST JULIAN C 12 c 2.2	SM

(73989) W4141—463. 400,000. 9/14. H.&J.Ltd. Forms/C. 2118/10.

Instructions regarding War Diaries and Intelligence Summaries are contained in F. S. Regs., Part II. and the Staff Manual respectively. Title pages will be prepared in manuscript.

WAR DIARY
or
~~INTELLIGENCE~~ SUMMARY.
(Erase heading not required.)

Army Form C. 2118.

503rd Field Coy RE

Hour, Date, Place	Summary of Events and Information	Remarks and references to Appendices
Reference Map Sheet 28 NW	1/20.000	
C22 b 7.0. 20. 9. 17	No 1 + 4 Section duckboard tracks toward ABRE (D7 a 75) and GENOA (D1 c 6 2) No 2 + 3 Section maintenance of footbridges across STEENBEEK. No 504571 L/Cpl FISHER F.W.G. + No 504634 Sap CALLAGHAN wounded No 504585 Sgt BRYANT A.G. + No 504468 L/Cpl FUSSELL	SM
" ~~21 9 17~~	Killed No 504492 L/Cpl SHELL E. No 504117 Sap RICE A. No 504155 Sgt BISHOP W.H. No 504338 Cpl ASHTON G.H. No 504043 Cpl SUTTON E. No 154401 Sap PARSONS H. No 504509 Sap ROUSELL T.R. + No 504515 Sap HARRIS R.H. wounded	
" 21 9 17	No 1 + 4 Section work on duckboard tracks, No 2 + 3 Section maintenance footbridges + ST JULIAN ROAD. No 504512 Sap MARCH W.H. wounded No 504576 Sap EDWARDS L.N. + No 504395 L/Cpl WILLIAMS G.V. wounded	SM SM
" 22 9 17	No. 1 + 4 Section duckboard tracks toward GENOA + ABRE. No 2 Section + No 3 Sect on shelters in CALIFORNIA TRENCH C 22 b 7 0	
" 23 9 17	No 1 + 4 Section duckboard track. No 1 Section completed track to GENOA. No 2 Section shelters. No 3 Section shelter. No 483412 Sap WARREN J.J. wounded	SM
" 24 9 17	No 1 + 4 Section duckboard track. No 2 + 3 Shelter. Coy shelled out of dugouts at 3.30 pm and 6.30 pm. 1 shelter destroyed, + 12 rifles bayonets + equipment No 504269 Cpl HOWES S. slightly wounded + remained at duty.	SM
" 25 9 17	Section on work as for 24th inst. No 504269 Cpl HOWES S gas burns + evacuated to CCS. Coy returned to Canal Bank at C25 d 3.5	SM
" 26 9 17	No 2 + 3 Section work on shelter in CALIFORNIA TRENCH. No 4 on duckboard tracks	SM
" 27 9 17	Coy moved from Canal Bank to BROWNE CAMP No 3 (A 22 b 8.4)	SM
A22 b 8.4 28 9 17	All sections physical training overhauling kit	SM
29 9 17	As for 28th. Packing wagons ready for move of transport	SM
" 30 9 17	Transport moved by road route to LOSTRAT halting for night at WORMHOUDT. Under command of Capt CHASEY, remainder of Coy Physical Training.	

S M Chapman Major
Cmdg 503 Fd Co RE

8

Instructions regarding War Diaries and Intelligence Summaries are contained in F. S. Regs., Part II. and the Staff Manual respectively. Title pages will be prepared in manuscript.

WAR DIARY
or
~~INTELLIGENCE SUMMARY.~~

(Erase heading not required.)

Army Form C. 2118.

503rd Field Coy R E

Vol 10

Hour, Date, Place		Summary of Events and Information	Remarks and references to Appendices
Ref Map Sheet 28 N.W. 1/20000		HAZEBROUCK + BELGIUM 1/100000	
A22. b 5.4.	1. 10 17	Unit left camp at 2.45 pm + marched to PESELHOEK (A20 d 5.3) + entrained for AUDRUICQ. 2A.9.5. detrained + marched to LOSTRAT 2A 2.1.	SM
LOSTRAT (2 A 2.1)	2. 10 17	Settling into billets	SM
"	3. 10 17	All section at training overhauling harness + Vehicles	SM
"	4 10 17	All Section at training. No 528648 Sap TILLETT. E reinforcement from RE Base Depot ROUEN	SM
"	5 10 17	All Section at training	SM
"	6 10 17	No 1 Section (Lt CHILTON) proceeded to NORDBECOURT 3.B.1.2 for work at X Corps Musketry School. No 2, 3 + 4 Section at training. No 504252 Sgt THOMPSON, S J, No 504325 LCpl GARDINER J B, No 504529 L Cpl HODGES H F, No 504470 L Cpl PORCH W, No 504327 Sapper BRONY A, No 504576 Sap EDWARDS [illegible] awarded Military Medal. (CRE orders No 18 dated 6.10.17)	SM
	7. 10 17	Church Parade	SM
	8. 10 17	No 2 Section employed on erecting NISSON Hut at NORDAUSQUES. No 3 + 4 Section Training. No 1 Section as on 6th 3 A 95 80.	SM
	9 10 17	As for 8th inst	SM
	10. 10 17	No 2 Section on Nissen Hut. No 3 + 4 Section moved to billet at BONNINGUES (3 A 2.5.) No 1 Section as on 6th construction of	SM
	11 10 17	No 2 Section on Nissen Hut. No 3 + 4 Section on Rifle Range at GUEMY (3 A 5.7.) Capt LE CHASET leave to ENGLAND. No 1 Section as on 6th inst	SM No 199411 Dr HALLYBONE, M.H. 142035 Sap RAW, N G 57900 " SHAW J F 536361 COLVILLE. T 470891 TRAYNER W 420092 GILBERT J reported from RE Base Depot ROUEN on 11.10.17 as reinforcements
	12 10 17	Work as for 11th inst.	SM
	13. 10 17	Work as for 11th inst	SM
	14 10 17	No work.	
	15 10 17	Hut at NORDAUSQUES finished. No 2 + 3 Section laying out training ground for Division at NORDAUSQUES	SM
	16. 10 17.	No 2 + 3 Section continued work on assault course. No 2 Section also commenced Hut for Div Sig. Train at ZUTKERQUE HAZEBROUCK Sheet 1/100000 2 A 25.12	

Instructions regarding War Diaries and Intelligence Summaries are contained in F. S. Regs., Part II. and the Staff Manual respectively. Title pages will be prepared in manuscript.

Army Form C. 2118.

WAR DIARY
or
~~INTELLIGENCE SUMMARY~~. 503rd Field Coy RE

(Erase heading not required.)

Hour, Date, Place	Summary of Events and Information	Remarks and references to Appendices
HAZEBROUCK [illegible]		
LOSTRAT 2A 2.1 17.10.17	No 2 Section [illegible] Hut at ZUTKERQUE ~~Bath at TOURNEHEM~~ (3A 6.6) No 3 & 4 Ranges at GUEMY. No 1 Section on detachment at NORTDECOURT 3B 1.3. No 8951 Pte WILLIAMS P reported on transfer to RE from 1st Bn HANTS Regt Authority D.A.G. 3rd Echelon CR No 38706/685/A dated 10.10.17)	SM
" 18.10.17	Work as for 17th inst	SM following reinforcements joined unit from RE Base Depot ROUEN on 18.10.17.
" 19.10.17	Sections withdrawn from BONNIGUES & NORTDECOURT. All vehicles packed ready for moving. ~~following reinforcements joined [illegible]~~	SM 552239 Sap JENNINGS J; 31085 " MARSH HA; 212513 " WILLAN J
20.10.17	Transport moved from LOSTRAT by march route to HOSPITAL FARM Camp Ref Map BELGIUM & FRANCE Sheet 28 B 19 d 2.2.	SM 398081 L/Cpl NOWELL W; 397896 Sap MAYALL A
HOSPITAL FARM 21.10.17	Dismounted Portion of Coy moved by rail from AUDRICQUES to HOPOUTRE, & marched to HOSPITAL FARM Camp.	SM 398073 " HILLOCK J; 396901 " McERLIVE D; 398435 " PARTRIDGE W
22.10.17	Settling into camp, unpacking stores & parking vehicles	SM 207852 " BOLTON A; 536297 " BISHOP H
23.10.17	No 1 Section erecting NISSEN HUTS No 2 attached to 171st Bde No 3 erecting horse standings & shelters No 4 Section overhauling all vehicles	SM 504576 " EDWARDS I H; 476776 " BINGHAM W; 430368 " HARKLEY H
24.10.17	Packing Vehicles ready for move	SM
" 25.10.17	moved into Shelters in CALEDONIA TRENCH C 15 a 7.6 Mounted Section & transport at HOSPITAL FARM. 1 officer &	SM Relieved 92nd Fd Coy RE in CALEDONIA TRENCH
CALEDONIA TRENCH C 15 a 7.6 26.10.17	50 O.R. Infantry of 175 Inf Bde reported for attachment to Coy	
10.17	No 1 Section work on Shelter at MINTY HOUSE No 2 & 4 on duckboard track to POELCAPPELLE. No 3 St JULIAN - POELCAPPELLE Road No 504329 Sap OLIVER JN wounded & evacuated to CCS on 26.10.17 No 107001 Pte HARDY H wounded do	SM
28.10.17	Work of Sections as for 27th inst	SM

(73989) W4141—463. 400,000. 9/14. H.&J.Ltd. Forms/C. 2118/10.

Instructions regarding War Diaries and Intelligence Summaries are contained in F. S. Regs., Part II. and the Staff Manual respectively. Title pages will be prepared in manuscript.

WAR DIARY
or
~~INTELLIGENCE~~ SUMMARY.
(*Erase heading not required.*)

503rd Fd Co RE

Army Form C. 2118.

Hour, Date, Place	Summary of Events and Information	Remarks and references to Appendices
CALADONIA TRENCH. 29.10.17 b 15. a 7.6	No 1 Section work on dressing station No 2 + 4 Section work on duckboard track to POELCAPPELLE, No 3 Section work on repair of ST JULIAN – POELCAPPELLE Rd.	Casualties 29.10.17 Lt J G COLLINS wounded 504223 Cpl. KNIGHT –"– 504470 2/Cpl PORCH H.J –"– 504552 Sap PHILLIPS. J.G –"– 504433 " HORNBDAH. –"– 504511 " BUSH. G.J –"– 504445 " FOLLEN H.A –"– 504467 " HIGHFIELD. F.J –"– 212573 " HILAN J –"–
30.10.17	No 1 Section work on dressing station, remainder no work on account of operations	
31.10.17	No 1 Section work on dressing station No 2 + 4 Sect on duckboard track No 3. ST JULIAN – POELCAPPELLE Rd	

S W Chapman Maj
OC 503 Fd Co RE

(73989) W4141—463. 400,000. 9/14. H.&J.Ltd. Forms/C. 2118/10.

Instructions regarding War Diaries and Intelligence Summaries are contained in F. S. Regs., Part II. and the Staff Manual respectively. Title pages will be prepared in manuscript.

WAR DIARY
or
~~INTELLIGENCE SUMMARY.~~ 503rd Fd Co RE

(*Erase heading not required.*)

Army Form C. 2118.

Vol 11

Reference Map Sheet 28 N.W. 1/20000

Hour, Date, Place		Summary of Events and Information	Remarks and references to Appendices
CALEDONIA TRENCH C.15.a.7.6.	1.11.17	No 1 Section work on dressing station at MINTY FARM & RUDOLPHE FARM No 2 Section repairing "N" duckboard track. No 3 Sect work on PHEASANT TRENCH (C.30.a.) No 4 Section construction of N. duckboard track towards HELLES HOUSES V.14.c.9.5.	Casualties 1.11.17 No 504576 Spr EDWARDS L.N. 495039 " CARTER A.B. Killed and No 99290 Spr ALDRIDGE T wounded.
	2.11.17	Sections work as on 1st inst.	No 182935 Spr RAW N.S. Killed 2.11.17 504044 Spr HOLBROOK H.A. 504402 " WHITE C.C. 504501 " TOOGOOD H.S. wounded on 2.11.17
	3.11.17	As above	
	4.11.17	As above except that No 4 Section commenced new duckboard track from BRENGRY V.20.a.5.7. to NOBLES FARM V.14.d.3.3. No 504155 Spr BISHOP W.H. reported as reinforcement from RE Base Depot ROUEN	552757 Spr REEVES D.N. gassed & admitted to Hospital on 3.11.17
	5.11.17	Work as on 4th inst.	
	6.11.17	As for 4th inst	504571 Cpl WARD R.J. gassed & admitted to hospital 5.11.17
	7.11.17	No work on account of operations	
	8.11.17	Work as for 4th inst. Duckboard track to NOBLES FARM completed. No 504445 L/Cpl ASHMAN H.H. 504502 Spr MARCH A. No 504415 Spr SMITH H. awarded Military Medal	504318 Cpl SMITH W.G. Killed 504465 Spr COBB E.H. wounded 6.11.17
	9.11.17	No 1 Section work on dressing station at MINTY FARM. No 2 repairing "N" duckboard track No 3 PHEASANT TRENCH No 4 N duckboard track to HELLES HOUSE V.14.c.8.6.	504495 L/Cpl LON H wounded 10.11.17
	10.11.17	As above	
	11.11.17	~~Work on~~ No 1 Section work at Bde HQ VARNA FARM, No 2 & 4 duckboard track No 3 PHEASANT TRENCH	504502 Spr MARCH A wounded on 12.11.17
	12.11.17	As for 11th inst	
	13.11.17	As for 11th inst No 504017 CSM HURST R.H.D. awarded the Distinguished Conduct Medal (CRE order No 25 d/13/11/17)	

(73989) W4141—463. 400,000. 9/14. H.&J.Ltd. Forms/C. 2118/10.

Instructions regarding War Diaries and Intelligence Summaries are contained in F. S. Regs., Part II. and the Staff Manual respectively. Title pages will be prepared in manuscript.

WAR DIARY
or
INTELLIGENCE SUMMARY.
(Erase heading not required.)

Army Form C. 2118.

Hour, Date, Place		Summary of Events and Information	Remarks and references to Appendices
Ref Map Sheet 28 NW		1/20.000	
CALEDONIA TRENCH C15a 7.6.	14 11/17	No 1 Section work at Bde HQ YARNA FARM. Shelters + track No 2 + 4 duckboard track, No 3 PHEASANT TRENCH.	SM
	15 11/17	Moved to Shelters in CANAL BANK C13 c 3.3.	
C13. c. 3.3	16 11/17	Packed ready to move. ~~T~~	
	17 11/17	Moved to HERZEELE area. Transport by road + dismounted portion by rail. Coy H.Q. at E7a 8.8. Sheet 27. NW	SM SM
Sheet 27. NW E7a 8.8.	18 11/17	Unpacking stores + settling into billets	SM
	19 11/17	Inspection of Arms, Clothing + Equipment + Sectional training	
	20 11/17	Sectional training	
	21 11/17	No 1 Section under Lt CHILTON proceeded to Corps workshops at ONDANK Sheet 28 A12 a 1.8. Nos 2, 3 + 4 Sectional training. Advance Party of Lt BILHAM + 3 other ranks proceeded to new area	SM
	22 11/17	Sectional Training - CRE visited Unit	SM
	23 11/17	Sectional Training + route march	SM
	24 11/17	Sectional Training + route march	SM
	25 11/17	Packing Vehicles ready for move	SM
	26 11/17	Sectional Training. Transport moved by road into new area	SM
	27 11/17	Coy marched to PROVEN entrained for ~~[illegible]~~ HIZGRNES Sheet 57 + marched to SANLIERES (L.C.8.5)	SM

Instructions regarding War Diaries and Intelligence Summaries are contained in F. S. Regs., Part II. and the Staff Manual respectively. Title pages will be prepared in manuscript.

WAR DIARY
or
~~INTELLIGENCE SUMMARY.~~ 503rd Fd Co RE

(*Erase heading not required.*)

Army Form C. 2118.

Hour, Date, Place	Summary of Events and Information	Remarks and references to Appendices
HAZEBROUCK Sheet 5A		
SAMETTE 28.11.17 (HQ 5 4)	Coy marched from SAMETTE to LONGUEVILLE (CALAIS Sheet 1/100,000 4 E 58) & billetted	SM
LONGUEVILLE 29.11.17 CALAIS SHEET 1/100,000 4 E 58	Settling into billets	
" 30.11.17	Overhauling stores cleaning vehicles & inspection of billets by CRE	SM
	S.H. Chapman Major [illegible] OC 503rd Field Coy RE	

(73989) W4141—463. 400,000. 9/14. H.&J.Ltd. Forms/C. 2118/10.

Instructions regarding War Diaries and Intelligence Summaries are contained in F.S. Regs., Part II. and the Staff Manual respectively. Title pages will be prepared in manuscript.

WAR DIARY
or
~~INTELLIGENCE SUMMARY.~~

(Erase heading not required.)

Army Form C. 2118.

503rd Fd Co RE

Vol 12

Hour, Date, Place		Summary of Events and Information	Remarks and references to Appendices
Ref Map CALAIS 1/100,000			
LONGUEVILLE 4 E 5.8.	1.12.17	Sectional Training	[illegible]
"	2.12.17	Church Parade at COLEMBERT	[illegible]
"	3.12.17	Sectional Training. Packing for move to SAMETTE	[illegible]
"	4.12.17	Moved by March route to SAMETTE Camp	[illegible]
SAMETTE	5.12.17	Transport moved by road. Dismounted portion of Coy at SAMETTE (Sheet 5A 4 B 4.4)	[illegible]
"	6.12.17	Embussed at LUMBRES for WIZERNES (4 C 8.5) & entrained for VLAMERTINGHE (2 J 8.3) & marched to billets in CANAL BANK (2 K 4 8.)	[illegible]
CANAL BANK 2 K 4 8. Sheet 5A	7.12.17	Settling into billets	[illegible]
	8.12.17	Taking over work of 205th Field Co RE. 3 Sections moved from CANAL BANK to Shelters in CANE POST. Capt CHASE [illegible] joined [illegible] School of Instruction for course	[illegible]
	9.12.17	No 1 Section Shelters in PHEASANT TRENCH, No 2 Shelters in CANE POST No 3 duckboard track, No 4 Horse Standings. Following men reported as reinforcements from RE Base Depot and are taken on strength from 4th December 1917 No 12407 [illegible] SMITH. H.C. No 183529 Sap MULLEN. G. No 84628 Sap MARSHALL. H.J. [No] 223014 Sap MORRIS. E. No 635165 Sap MILLER. A. No 216695 Sap MOORE T. No 285249 Sap MERRILL. H. No 187779 Sap MADERVILLE [illegible] No [illegible] Sap MORTIMORE No 108904 Sap CHAPMAN. T.H. No 91302 Sap BIRCH. R. No 339[illegible] Sap LEE. A.E. No 118398 Sap BANSON G.E. No 277309 Sap GOZAR J. No 202[illegible] Sap [illegible] No 300[illegible] Sap JARRETT [illegible]	[illegible]
	10.12.17	Work as for 9th inst. Following reinforcements reported from RE Base Depot & are taken on strength from 7th inst No 131650 Sap GOODWIN J.L. No 108737 Sap JONES B. No 496[illegible] Sap RICH T.H. No 402807 Sap TREIL H.	[illegible]

(73989) W4141—463. 400,000. 9/14. H.&J.Ltd. Forms/C. 2118/10.

Instructions regarding War Diaries and Intelligence Summaries are contained in F. S. Regs., Part II. and the Staff Manual respectively. Title pages will be prepared in manuscript.

WAR DIARY
or
INTELLIGENCE SUMMARY.
(Erase heading not required.)

Army Form C. 2118.

503rd Fd Co RE

Hour, Date, Place	Summary of Events and Information	Remarks and references to Appendices
Ref Map HAZEBROUCK	Sheet 5a	
CANAL BANK 11.12.17 2 K 4.8	Work of sections as for 9th inst. Following reinforcements were taken on strength 10.12.17 No 223968 Sr CANTON J.H. & 504412 Dr RUMMINGS A. from RE Base Depot	[illegible]
12.12.17	Work of Section as for 9th inst	[illegible]
13.12.17	No 1 Section PHEASANT TRENCH & duckboard track No 2 Section duckboard track No 3 Section Platoon Posts in front line No 4 Section Hutting & Shelters	[illegible]
14.12.17	Work as for 13th	[illegible]
15.12.17	Work as for 13th	[illegible]
16.12.17	Work as for 13th Sites selected for 4 defensive Post by CRE	[illegible]
17.12.17	Work of Sections as for 13th. Site of one work traced	[illegible]
18.12.17	Work as for 13th - Sites of 2 works on Corps line traced - & one drained. Front sector	CAG
19.12.17	Work as for 13th Tracing line of wire round POELCAPELLE by no 3 Section -	CAG
20.12.17	No 1 Section - Duckboards - No 2 - Platoon Posts in Front line - No 3 Horse-lines - Hutting & Shelters - No 4 PHEASANT TRENCH & posts and duckboards - Excavation of Post begun -	CAG
21.12.17	Work as for 20th No 3 & 4 Sites in Corps line traced -	CAG
22.12.17	No 1 Section Work on GLOSTER AV. duckboarding from No 4 - otherwise work as on 20th. Tracing line of wire round POELCAPELLE continued by No 2 - Night work generally stopped by enemy shelling -	CAG
23.12.17	Work as on 22nd 4 Platoon Posts round NORFOLK Ho traced - Tracing line of wire round POELCAPELLE completed - No 2 & 4 with Sapping Platoons started wiring there -	CAG
24.12.17	Work as on 23rd - A third Sapping Platoon added to POELCAPELLE wiring party - Thaw set in -	CAG

(73989) W4141—463. 400,000. 9/14. H.&J.Ltd. Forms/C. 2118/10.

Instructions regarding War Diaries and Intelligence Summaries are contained in F. S. Regs., Part II. and the Staff Manual respectively. Title pages will be prepared in manuscript.

WAR DIARY

or

~~INTELLIGENCE SUMMARY.~~ 503rd Field Co R.E.

(Erase heading not required.)

Army Form C. 2118.

Hour, Date, Place	Summary of Events and Information	Remarks and references to Appendices
25.12.17	Work as for 22nd Snow	CAC
26.12.17	Work as for 22nd Snow & frost. Night work impeded by Shell fire	CAC
27.12.17	No 1 Section took on from No 2 – No 2 Section took on from No 3 – No 3 Section took on from No 1 – No 4 continued –	CAC
		CAC
28.12.17	Work as for 27th	CAC
29.12.17	Work as for 27th	CAC
30.12.17	Work as for 27th except no Night work	CAC
31.12.17	Work as for 27th	

C. Chasey Capt
for Major
503 (Wessex) Fd. Coy. R.E.

Instructions regarding War Diaries and Intelligence Summaries are contained in F. S. Regs., Part II. and the Staff Manual respectively. Title pages will be prepared in manuscript.

WAR DIARY ~~or INTELLIGENCE SUMMARY.~~

(56)

(*Erase heading not required.*)

Army Form C. 2118.

503rd Field Co R E

WO 95/3

Ref Map Sheet S.A.

Hour, Date, Place	Summary of Events and Information	Remarks and references to Appendices
CANAL BANK 2.K 4.8. 1.1.18	Work ~~of~~ of Sections No 1 Section No 2 & No 3 Section wiring POELCAPPELLE No 4 Section [illegible] wiring Corps Line	[illegible]
" 2.1.18	Work as for 1st [illegible] The following officers N.C.O. & Sappers were mentioned in [illegible] Despatch of Nov 7th 1917 Major S [illegible] No 50[illegible] CSM B. HORST. No 504512 Sapper C T HARWICK. No 12[illegible] S.P. J PEARSON [illegible] Major S [illegible] CHAPMAN [illegible] for leave to U.K.	[illegible]
3.1.18	Work of Sections No 2 3 & 4 wiring POELCAPPELLE No 1 Section [illegible] CANE POST Work on Corps Line under supervision of OC No 2 [illegible]	[illegible]
4.1.18	Work of Sections ~~[illegible]~~ wiring [illegible] [illegible]	[illegible]
5.1.18	Work of Sections as for 4th [illegible] on leave to UK	[illegible]
6.1.18	Work of Sections as for 4th [illegible] 175th Infantry Brigade [illegible]	[illegible]
7.1.18	Work of Sections as for 4th [illegible]	[illegible]
8.1.18	Handed over work to 508th Field Coy [illegible] took over work on Corps Line [illegible] moved billets to E bank of CANAL [illegible] from 511th & 5[illegible] Coy RE	[illegible]
9.1.18	No 1 & 2 Sections wiring on Corps Line No 3 [illegible] No 4 Section Coy [illegible]	[illegible]

(73989) W4141—463. 400,000. 9/14. H.&J.Ltd. Forms/C. 2118/10.

Instructions regarding War Diaries and Intelligence Summaries are contained in F. S. Regs., Part II. and the Staff Manual respectively. Title pages will be prepared in manuscript.

WAR DIARY

or

INTELLIGENCE SUMMARY.

(Erase heading not required.)

503rd Fd Coy RE

Army Form C. 2118.

Hour, Date, Place	Summary of Events and Information	Remarks and references to Appendices
Ref Map Sheet 5 A		
CANAL BANK 21 K 4.8 10/1/18	No 1 2 + 4 Section wiring on Corps Line No 3 Section Coy Employ	SM
11/1/18	As for 10th inst	SM
12/1/18	As for 10th inst except that No 1, 2 + 4 Section were employed on concrete shelters in addition to wiring	SM
13/1/18	No 1, 2 + 4 Section concrete shelters, wiring No 3 Section Coy work	SM
14/1/18	No 1 2 + 4 Section wiring No 3 Coy Employ	SM
15/1/18	As for 14th	SM
16/1/18	As for 14th inst	SM
17/1/18	Coy moved by rail to billets at PROVEN (Sheet 27. E12 d 2.7.)	SM
PROVEN (Sheet 27, E12d27) 18/1/18	Settling into billets cleaning vehicles	SM
19/1/18	Loading Stores + packing vehicles for move	SM
20/1/18 21/1/18	Moved by rail from PROVEN to VILLERS-BRETTONEUX (AMIENS Sheet 2 G) marched to billets at AUBIGNY (AMIENS SHEET 2 F 7.8	SM
AUBIGNY (AMIENS SHEET 2 F.7.8) 22/1/18	Settling into billets, unpacking vehicles + cleaning them	SM
" 23/1/18	Packing vehicles ready for move	SM
ROSIERES (3 I 5.8) 24/1/18	Moved by march route to ROSIERES + went into billets for the night	SM
ROYE (4.J. 5.4) 25/1/18	Moved by march route to ROYE + went into billets for the night	SM
OGNOLLES 4.K.(95.40) 26/1/18	Moved by march route to OGNOLLES + went into billets for the night	SM
NEUFLIEUX (ST QUENTIN SHEET 5.B9.5) 27/1/18	Moved by march route to NEUFLIEUX (ST QUENTIN SHEET 5 B 9.5)	SM
" 28/1/18	Resting in billets. Took over from FRENCH ENGINEERS documents relating to destruction of bridges over the CANAL de ST QUENTIN.	SM

(73989) W4141—463. 400,000. 9/14. H.&J.Ltd. Forms/C. 2118/10.

Army Form C. 2118.

Instructions regarding War Diaries and Intelligence Summaries are contained in F. S. Regs., Part II. and the Staff Manual respectively. Title pages will be prepared in manuscript.

WAR DIARY
~~or~~
~~INTELLIGENCE SUMMARY.~~ 503rd Fd Coy R.E

(*Erase heading not required.*)

Place	Date	Hour	Summary of Events and Information	Remarks and references to Appendices
NEUFLIEUX ST QUENTIN Sheet 5 B.9.5	29/1/18		No 1 + 3 Section moved to billets at TERGUIER (5 D 5.8) H.Q + No 2 + 4 Section, remain at NEUFLIEUX	F.M.
"	30/1/18		No 1 + 3 Section Improvement of billet at TERGUIER. Nos 2 + 4 Section moved to NOREUIL ( )	F.M.
"	31/1/18		All section on improvements of billets. No 2 + 4 Section at work on NOREUIL + VIRY NOREUIL.	F.M.

F.N. Chapman Major
O.C. 503rd Fd Coy RE

Instructions regarding War Diaries and Intelligence Summaries are contained in F. S. Regs., Part II. and the Staff Manual respectively. Title pages will be prepared in manuscript.

WAR DIARY
or
~~INTELLIGENCE SUMMARY.~~
(Erase heading not required.)

Army Form C. 2118.

503rd Fd Co RE

VII 14

Place	Date	Hour	Summary of Events and Information	Remarks and references to Appendices
Ref Map			ST QUENTIN + SHEET 70D	
NEUFLIEUX ST QUENTIN Sheet 5 B9.5 — 1 —	1.2.18		No 1 & 3 Section improvement of accommodation at TERGNIER (5 D 5.8) + No 2 & 4 Sections improvement of accommodation at NOREUIL + VIRY NOREUIL	SM
	2.2.18		Coy HQ & transport moved to VIRY NOREUIL (Sheet 70 D. A16 a 3 5) Sections working as on 1st Feb.	SM
VIRY NOREUIL Sheet 70 D. A16 a 3 5)	3.2.18		Nos 1 + 3 Sections improvement of accommodation at TERGNIER + No 2 + 4 Sections at VIRY, NOREUIL.	SM
	4.2.18		As for 3rd Feb	SM
	5.2.18		No 1 + 3 Work on defences improvement of trenches. No 2 + 4 improvement of accommodation at VIRY NOREUIL. IILieut E. BILHAM proceeded to UK on leave	SM
	6.2.18		As for 5th inst. The following reported as reinforcement from R.E. Base Depot: 504325 Sgt GARDINER J.B. – 103425 Spr HUNTER H. 504419 Dr WILBRAHAM E.G.	SM
	7.2.18		No 1 & 3 Section:– Work on defences Corps Line:– No. 2 Section. Improvement of accommodation at VIRY NOUREUIL. No 4 Section: Building Trestle Bridge over ST QUENTIN CANAL at A23a 33 (Sheet 70D)	[illegible]
	8.2.1918		As on 7th inst. Major S.W. CHAPMAN proceeded to G.H.Q. R.E School. BLENDECQUES for course of instruction. Lieut. F.G. BANKS & 504448 Cpl ASHMAN W.H. proceeded to V Army School of Infantry Training TOUTENCOURT for course of instruction	[illegible]
	9.2.1918		Nos 1.3 & 4 Sections As on 8th – No 2 Section – Preparing bridges for demolition on ST QUENTIN CANAL between T14 d 44 (66c Sheet) & B7c 78 (Sheet 70D)	[illegible]
	10.2.1918		Nos 1.3 & 4 Sections As on 9th – No 2 Section Moved from NOUREUIL into TERGNIER. Work on bridges as 9th	[illegible]
	11.2.1918		As on 10th inst	[illegible]
	12.2.1918		As on 11th inst.– Lieut AVIS P.S from 511th Field Company RE attached for duty	[illegible]
	13.2.1918		As on 12th inst. No 504291 Farrier Sgt VAGE proceeded to No 7 Vet Hospital for course of instruction.	[illegible]
	14.2.1918		As on 13th inst.	[illegible]
	15.2.1918		Nos 1.2 & 3 Sections as on 14th. No 4 Section Improving billets at VIRY-NOUREUIL – repairing water supply at Hospital CHAUNY.	[illegible]

A5834 Wt. W4973/M687 750,000 8/16 D. D. & L. Ltd. Forms/C.2118/13.

Instructions regarding War Diaries and Intelligence Summaries are contained in F. S. Regs., Part II. and the Staff Manual respectively. Title pages will be prepared in manuscript.

WAR DIARY
or
INTELLIGENCE SUMMARY. 503rd Field Co. R.E.

(Erase heading not required.)

Army Form C. 2118.

Place	Date	Hour	Reference Maps: ST QUENTIN 66c 70D — Summary of Events and Information	Remarks and references to Appendices
VIRY NOUREUIL	16.2.1918		Nos 2 & 3 Sections - Preparing bridges for demolition as 15th. Nos 1 & 4 Improving billets in morning. No 4 Section moved from NOUREUIL and relieved No 1 Section at TERGNIER - No 1 Section moved from TERGNIER and relieved No 4 Section at NOUREUIL. Rehearsal of demolition of bridges in afternoon.	[initials]
	17.2.1918		No 1 Section - Improving stables at VIRY NOUREUIL. Nos 2 & 3 Sections as 16th inst - No 4 Section Improving billets at TERGNIER. The following reinforcements reported from Base Depot. 202912 Spr KITSON E.D. 231103 BUCKINGHAM B - 130213 Spr BIDDLE F - 203911 Spr ALLEN W - 138770 Spr TAYLOR A.E. - 135374 Spr WALKER T - 231689 Spr WATTS W.H. - 515132 Spr SAWDEN H - 514967 Spr BACK E.J - 514250 Spr BRASNGQ S.E. - 171807 Spr FOX [illegible] - 541810 Spr PATTISON H - 402334 Spr DAVIDSON G -	[initials]
	18.2.1918		No 1 Section as on 17th inst - No 2 Section - Erecting screens on [illegible] - FARGNIER Road. - No 3 Section Work on defences at TRAVECY [illegible] (66c) - No 4 Section work on defences at T 2 b 22 - T 4 d 59 T 24 d 42 (66c). Lieut S.A. CHILTON proceeded to R.E. Base for M.3. ([illegible] M 326 [illegible] 18.2.18)	[initials]
	19.2.1918		Sections As on 18th.	[initials]
	20.2.1918		Sections as on 19th	[initials]
	21.2.1918		Sections as on 20th	[initials]
	22.2.1918		Sections as on 21st. II Lieut E. [illegible]HAM returned from leave to U.K. - The following reinforcements [illegible] from Base Depot. No. 223283 Spr PARKES W. - 385334 Spr GRIFFITHS G. - 134132 Spr BAIRD C.B. -	[initials]
	23.2.1918		Sections Nos. 1. 2 & 4 as on 22nd inst. No 3 Section - Constructing Batt. Hd Qrs in spoil bank at T 2 c 35.10. (Sheet 66c)	[initials]
	24.2.1918		Nos. 1.3 & 4 Section as on 23rd inst. No 2 Section. Repairing dams on Causeway at B19a11 - B19c29 - B19d58 - B19a76 (Sheet 70D).	[initials]
	25.2.1918		Sections as on 24th inst	[initials]
	26.2.1918		Sections Nos 1. 2 & 3 as 25th inst. No 4 Section Work on defences Battle Zone. - No 304291 Farrier Sergt [illegible] returned from course	[initials]
	27.2.1918		Sections as on 26th inst.	[initials]
	28.2.1918		Sections as on 27th inst. Wire received at 1.30pm from C.R.E. 58th Division - W.5 [illegible] 28.2.1918. Ordering [illegible] parties to be withdrawn, and Sections to stand by at Company Hd. Qrs. - All sappers less those detailed for demolition of bridges returned to NOUREUIL at 6pm.	[initials]

A5834 Wt. W4973/M687 750,000 8/16 D. D. & L. Ltd. Forms/C.2118/13.

[signature] Major,
Commanding 503rd (Wessex) Fd. Coy. R.E.

Instructions regarding War Diaries and Intelligence Summaries are contained in F. S. Regs., Part II. and the Staff Manual respectively. Title pages will be prepared in manuscript.

WAR DIARY
or
INTELLIGENCE SUMMARY. 503rd Field Co. R.E.

(*Erase heading not required.*)

Army Form C. 2118.

Place	Date	Hour	Summary of Events and Information — Reference Maps { ST. QUENTIN 66c 70D.	Remarks and references to Appendices
VIRY NOUREUIL (Sheet 70D) (A16a 1.7)	1.3.1918		Wire received at 1.30 am from C.R.E. 58th Division No: W.13. Resume normal conditions. – All sappers withdrawn on 28.2.1918 returned to billets at TERGNIER. Practice of Manning Battle Stations carried out in accordance with C.R.E. 58 Division No W.17 dated 1.3.18	[illegible]
	2.3.1918		No 1 Section – Work on defences Battle Zone. No 2 Section – Repairing dams CONDREN Causeway at B19b11 – B19d29 – B19d58 & B19d76 (Sheet 70D) – No 3 Section Constructing Battalion Hd Qrs in Spoil Bank at T1a 35.10 (Sheet 66c) No 4 Section – ~~Erecting~~ Fixing Gas Blankets – Testing charges on Bridges.	[illegible]
	3.3.1918		Work as for 2nd. Major S.N. CHAPMAN returned from RE course at BLENDECQUES.	SM
	4.3.18		Work as for 2nd	SM
	5.3.18		Work as for 2nd No 504525 Cpl E C RICHARDS proceeded to Bridging School AIRE for course of instruction	SM
	6.3.18		Work as for 2nd	SM
	7.3.18		Do – Do –	SM
	8.3.18		Work as for 2nd. 2Lt G H MENTZ reported for duty	SM
	9.3.18		Work as for 2nd	SM
	10.3.18		Do Do No 504040 L Cpl HINCHWORTH. E } 504520 Sap WILTSHIRE. F } proceeded to BASE DEPOT. FOREWAY [illegible] [illegible] SAVY authority DAG 3rd Echelon CR 35335/[illegible] dated 7.3.18	SM
	11.3.18		Do Do	SM
	12.3.18		No 1 Section Work on wire in Battle Zone. No 2 Section Repairing dams at CONDREN. No 3 Batt HQ, RAP at VOUEL. No 4 Section Shelters in front line & fixing gas blankets	SM
	13.3.18		Work as for 12th	SM
	14.3.18		Work as for 12th	SM
	15.3.18		Work as for 12th	SM
	16.3.18		Work as for 12	SM
	17.3.18		Work as for 12th. 2Lt Banks No 504445 Cpl ASHMAN W.H. returned from course at [illegible]COURT Fifth Army Infantry School of Instruction	SM
	18.3.18		Work as for 12th	SM
	19.3.18		Work as for 12th 2Lt BANKS proceeded on leave [illegible]	SM

A5834 Wt. W4973/M687 750,000 8/16 D. D. & L. Ltd. Forms/C.2118/13.

9

Instructions regarding War Diaries and Intelligence Summaries are contained in F. S. Regs., Part II. and the Staff Manual respectively. Title pages will be prepared in manuscript.

WAR DIARY
or
~~INTELLIGENCE SUMMARY.~~ 503rd Fd Co RE

58 Div

(Erase heading not required.)

Vol 15

Army Form C. 2118.

Place	Date	Hour	Summary of Events and Information	Remarks and references to Appendices
			Reference Map ST QUENTIN 66C & 70D & 70E	
VIRY NOUREUIL 70D 2.1.5 a 1.7.	20.3.18		Orders received to "prepare for attack" followed by MAN BATTLE STATIONS. Personnel detailed for demolition of bridges under Lt NAGG & 2Lt BILHAM dealt accordingly	SWC
	21.3.18		Bridge 19 to 24 & 26 & footbridge P.Q.R.S.T.U.V & X, over the ST QUENTIN CANAL were demolished. No 25 bridge not demolished by order of 41173rd Inf Bde. Coy acted with Infantry Bde in repelling enemy attack on TERGNIER (ST QUENTIN Sheet 66C) S.C. 5.2.	SWC
	22.3.18		~~Killed No 398566 Sap ARMITAGE. B.S.~~ SWC. Wounded 2Lt BILHAM E.J (remained on duty) No 504519 Sap HOBBS G. No 504572 Cpl WESTBURY. E. No 504507 L/Cpl MULCOCK H. No 426575 Sap BAXTER. A. No 504301 Sap FLINT. W.J. No 224574 Sap JACKSON H. ~~Following casualties~~	SWC
	23.3.18		Coy acting as Infantry. Took up position in line at A 15 c 5 2 & continued in action in any occupied position along E bank of CANAL at L.15.d 9.5 & L 16 c 2 9. Following casualties recorded. Wounded No 504360 Sap FROST. H No 504457 Sap MAYNARD S H No 105737 Sap JONES. B. No 250942 Sap KING. L G No 504469 Sap TANNER H F. 395073 " WILCOX. J. 105737 " CHAPMAN T 139653 " GOODWIN. J. 184745 " MORTIMER H. Killed No 398566 Sap ARMITAGE B.S	SWC
BESME R14 b 9.5.	24.3.18		Coy ~~[illegible]~~ marched to BESME Sheet 70E R14 b 9.5. & constructed strong points at R7.a.1.6 R8.b 4.[illegible] L 33.c. Casualties No 277309 Sap POYZER J.A. No 440391 L/Cpl TRAYNOR W. 224439 Sap OGDEN [illegible] 503263 SHEET 6	SWC
	25.3.18		Work on defences.	SWC
	26.3.18		Constructing bridge for Infantry in file over canal at L 36 a 8.1. Bridges at MANICAMP prepared for demolition	SWC
	27.3.18		Bridge at L 29 a 2.9. prepared for demolition. No 504514 Sap LOVE G.H. No 3469 [illegible] McFARLANE C wounded	
	28.3.18		Work on defences between MANICAMP L 27 & BOIS DE MANICAMP L 35 a & c. ~~[illegible]~~	SWC
	29.3.18		Work on defences as for 28th. No 2 section Shelters for Battalion HQ in BOIS DE FEVS at R10 c 5.5.	SWC
	30.3.18		No 1 Section work on defences, No 2 & 3. Shelter for Bde HQ at R10 b. No 4 Section working on AILETTE Bn between MANICAMP. & L ~~29~~ ~~a~~ 30 c 01.30	SWC
	31.3.18		Work as for 30th. General FERAUD Commanding 1st French Cavalry Corps expressed his appreciation of good work done by Engineers of Division. Copy of letter forwarded to Units under CRE 58 Division No 32922 dated 30.3.18	SWC

S.W. Chapman Maj
OC 503rd Fd Co RE
31/3/18

A5834 Wt. W4973/M687 750,000 8/16 D. D. & L. Ltd. Forms/C.2118/13.

58th Div.

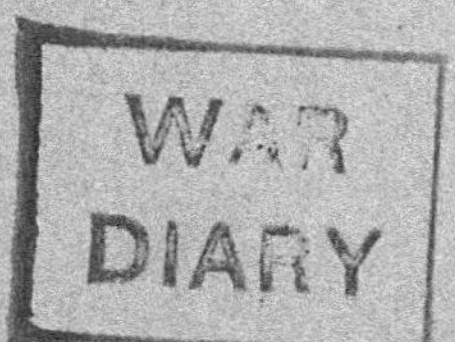

503rd FIELD COMPANY, R.E.

A P R I L

1 9 1 8

4

Instructions regarding War Diaries and Intelligence Summaries are contained in F. S. Regs., Part II. and the Staff Manual respectively. Title pages will be prepared in manuscript.

WAR DIARY
or
~~INTELLIGENCE SUMMARY~~. 503rd Fd Co RE

(Erase heading not required.)

Army Form C. 2118.

Vol 16

Place	Date	Hour	Ref Map Sheet 70 E. SOISSONS. 1/100.000 AMIENS. 1/100.000 Summary of Events and Information	Remarks and references to Appendices
BESME R14 b 9.5	1.4.18		No 1 Section work on defence line MANICAMP L 29 b to BOIS DE MANICAMP L 35 b. No 2 & 3 Sections erection of shelters for Bde & Bty HQ at R 10 c & R 16 b. No 4 Section wiring N bank of AILETTE River & strong Point at L 30 c 5.4.	[illegible]
BLERANCOURT	2.4.18		Work as for 1st inst. Orders received from CRE 58th Division to withdraw charges in bridges at MANICAMP before handing over to FRENCH ENGINEERS who would use their own explosives. Handed over work to the FRENCH, & Coy marched to BLERANCOURT R 31 a & went into caves at X 2 d 3.4	SM
LE MESNIL	3.4.18		Marched to LE MESNIL & went into billets for the night	SM
AMBLENY	4.4.18		Marched to AMBLENY & went into billets for the night	SM
DOMMIERS	5.4.18		Marched to DOMMIERS & went into billets for the night	SM
2E 5 B.	6.4.18		Marched to LONGPONT & entrained for LONGUEAU (2.E.2.5) & went into [illegible] at 2E 5 B	SM
AMIENS SHEET	7.4.18		No 2 & 4 Section strengthening cellars at CHATEAU M 36 central (Sheet 62 D) No 1 & 3 making shelters	SM
	8.4.18		No 1 & 2 Sections moved to VILLERS BRETTONEUX for work on wiring. No 3 & 4 Sections work on CHATEAU, sandbagging windows. Capt G H NORRIS reported for duty from 511th Fd Coy RE	SM
	9.4.18		Work as for 8th inst. Lt E WALL attached to HQ 178th Inf Bde for liaison purposes.	SM
	10.4.18		Work as for 8th inst. No 4 Section moved to VILLERS BRETTONEUX to work on Bn HQ	SM
	11.4.18		No 1 Section returned to Coy HQ after work. No 2 & 4 Section work on wiring & Bn HQ at VILLERS BRETTONEUX. No 3 Section work at CHATEAU (M 36 central Sheet 62 D.)	SM
	12.4.18		No 3 Section proceeded to & No 2 Section returned from VILLERS BRETTONEUX. Work as for 11th inst for No 4 Section. No 1 Section resting	SM
	13.4.18		Handed over work to 511th Fd Co RE & took over from 511th Fd Co RE work on Reserve line BOIS D'ABBE to U 15 b 8.8.	SM
	14.4.18		No 1 Section wiring. No 2 Section constructing shelters in BOIS D'AMIE. No 3 Section wiring No 4 Section Bn & Coy HQrs	SM
	15.4.18		As for 14th	SM
	16.4.18		As for 14	SM
	17.4.18		As for 14th	SM
	18.4.18		Took over work from 504th Fd Co RE on Reserve line right Section from BOIS DE GENTELLES to BOIS DE [illegible]	SM

A5834 Wt. W4973/M687 750,000 8/16 D. D. & L. Ltd. Forms/C.2118/13.

Instructions regarding War Diaries and Intelligence Summaries are contained in F. S. Regs., Part II. and the Staff Manual respectively. Title pages will be prepared in manuscript.

WAR DIARY
or
~~INTELLIGENCE~~ SUMMARY. 503rd (Wessex) Field Co. R.E.

(*Erase heading not required.*)

Place	Date	Hour	Summary of Events and Information	Remarks and references to Appendices
			Reference Maps:- AMIENS 1/100.000; SHEET 62D S.W. 1/20.000; LENS 1/100.000	
1½ miles East of CACHY at M36d52 (Sheet 62D)	19·4·1918		No 1 Section Wiring at O32 (Sheet 62D) – No 2 Section Wiring at U7 & U.13 (Sheet 62D) – No 3 Section – Excavating trenches in T30c (Sheet 62D) – No 4 Section Fixing gas blankets VILLERS BRETONNEUX – The following N.C.O & Sappers wounded. 504525 Corpl RICHARDS E.C (remained at duty) 216695 Sapper MOORE T. – (died of wounds on 20th) 231109 Sapper BUCKINGHAM. B. (evacuated)	L.C.C.
	20·4·1918		No 1 Section as on 19th – No 2 Section Excavating trench - CACHY SWITCH – U7d – U8c – U8b – U8d – (Sheet 62D) No 3 Section as on 19th – No 4 Section Excavating for 2 Battn Hd Qrs at T17c72 – (62D)	L.C.C.
	21·4·1918		Nos 1, 2, 3 & 4 Sections as on 20th	L.C.C.
	22·4·1918		Nos 1·2·3 & 4 Sections as on 21st	L.C.C.
	23·4·1918		No 1 Section Fixing gas blankets to dug outs at U1a80 & U7a62. Nos 2-3 & 4 Sections as on 22nd – The following N.C.O & Sapper reported as reinforcements 504597 L/Cpl MULCOCK A.E. – 143636 Sapper KEMPIN L.W	L.C.C.
	24·4·1918		Company stood to. – Major S.W CHAPMAN and Lieut. E WALL awarded M.C. No 504359 Corpl A. TUCKER awarded D.C.M. III Corps R.O No 247 – 24th Apl 1918.	L.C.C.
	25·4·1918		Nos 1 & 3 Sections proceeded at 11.30 p.m. to support trenches for work on consolidating front line in BOIS de HANGARD after attack – under orders of B.G.C 53rd Infy Brigade.	L.C.C.
	26·4·1918		No 2 & 4 Sections Wiring front line, BOIS de HANGARD. Lieut T. G. BANKS RE. Killed – 2/Lieut G. W. MENTZ wounded and evacuated.	L.C.C.
	27·4·1918		Company proceeded by March route to AMIENS and from there to COULONVILLERS (Lens 5A17) by bus. Transport staging night at LE MESGE (AMIENS 1A6.4).	L.C.C.
COULONVILLERS. (LENS. 5A17)	28·4·1918		Cleaning billets – preparing cookhouses &c. Transport arrived in afternoon.	L.C.C.
	29·4·1918		Cleaning vehicles. – Arms inspection.	L.C.C.
	30·4·1918		Kit inspection:-	L.C.C.

L.C. Chasey Capt.
~~Major~~
Commanding 503rd (Wessex) Fd. Coy. R.E.

A5834 Wt. W4973/M687 750,000 8/16 D. D. & L. Ltd. Forms/C.2118/13.

7 CONFIDENTIAL Vol 17

WAR DIARY.

OF

503RD FIELD COY. R.E

FROM 1-5-18 TO 31-5-18

VOL. 17.

Army Form C. 2118.

Instructions regarding War Diaries and Intelligence Summaries are contained in F. S. Regs., Part II. and the Staff Manual respectively. Title pages will be prepared in manuscript.

WAR DIARY
or
~~INTELLIGENCE SUMMARY.~~

(Erase heading not required.)

503rd (WESSEX) FIELD CO: R.E.

Ref Map LENS 11 1/100,000

Place	Date	Hour	Summary of Events and Information	Remarks and references to Appendices
COULENVILLERS (LENS 5.A1.7)	1.5.18		Coy Training. Drill etc. Undermentioned reinforcements arrived from RE Base Depot 584653 L Cpl PAYNE L; 277820 Sap FISHER H; 488172 " DAVIES; 304586 " CALVERT J; 83797 " BANNISTER J; 26777 " CRANFORD J 494038 Sap GOULD P; 434289 " JOHNSON H; 412794 " BROWN W; 216624 " VAUGHAN P; 23878 " MORRISON T; 11125 " JONES A 205585 Sap MIDSON S; 471436 " McNAB S; 93466 " DAVIDSON M; 518763 " WEBBER N; 69444 " MORRIS A; 67081 " THOMPSON A 141667 Sap GARRETT W; 89878 " BEENET B; 48782 " SWEETMAN; 145720 " VICKERS F; 92837 " HILL J G; 466390 " LAWSON J 388840 Sap FLETCHER A; 398456 " GAIR J; 70374 2/Cpl LEETH T; 477104 L/Cpl LEHANE P; 30702 Dr WILLIAMS; 305045 " GOMM T	SM
"	2.5.18		Coy Training	SM
"	3.5.18		Coy Training. No 504359 Cpl A TUCKER awarded the CROIX DE GUERRE 1st class (dated 1.5.18)	SM
"	4.5.18		No 1, 2, 3, 4 Section fired musketry course of 25 rounds.	SM
"	5.5.18		Church Parade. ~~[illegible]~~ Mounted portion moved by march route to BRAIZIEUX (62D NW C.11.9.7)	SM
BRAIZIEUX	6.5.18		Dismounted portion moved by bus to BRAIZIEUX (62D NW C.11.9.7) & billeted.	SM
"	7.5.18		Moved into bivouac in BOIS DE ROBERT C.11.C.9.3. Nos 1-2-3 & 4 Section work on Bde HQ at C.17.a.7.7. digging shelters.	SM
	8.5.18		No 1, 2, 3, 4 Section work on Bde HQ. Lt D.A. BEVIS 511th 3rd CRE attached for duty on 7th. Lt R. KINGDON, "Lt BO ALDOUS. No 504359 Cpl TUCKER & 504529 L/Cpl HODGES H.E. & No 495093 Sap FOSTER A reported as reinforcements from RE Base Depot	SM
	9.5.18		No 1-2-3 & 4 Section work on Bde HQ and Bn HQ for 10th & 12th Bn	SM
	10.5.18		No 1-2-3 Section on trenches in Reserve Line from D19 central to D1a. No 4 Section on Bde & Bn HQ. Lt D.A. BEVIS rejoined 511th 3rd CRE	SM
	11.5.18		Work as for 10th	SM
	12.5.18		Work as for 10th	SM
	13.5.18		No 1 & 3 Section work on Reserve line. No 2 Section wiring & No 4 Sect. accommodation for Bn HQ	SM
	14.5.18		No 1.2 & 3 Sect. work on Reserve line. No 4 Sect. accommodation.	SM
	15.5.18		No 1.2 & 3 Sect. work on Reserve line. No 4 Sec. accommodation. Reconnaissance of line by OC & Lt HALL, KINGDON & 2/Lt ALDOUS. A/Capt (act Capt) G.H. NORRIS joined 214th AT Coy RE. No 504.599 Cpl FISHER E, No 422504 L Cpl RAE H, No 57191 Sap DANBY L, No 474148 Sap GOSLING A, No 471357 Sap ATKINSON L joined from 213 AT Coy RE (Cpl FISHER from RE Base Depot)	SM

(A7092). Wt W12839/M1293. 75,000. 1/17. D. D. & L., Ltd. Forms/C.2118/14.

Instructions regarding War Diaries and Intelligence Summaries are contained in F. S. Regs., Part II. and the Staff Manual respectively. Title pages will be prepared in manuscript.

WAR DIARY
or
INTELLIGENCE SUMMARY.
(Erase heading not required.)

Army Form C. 2118.

503rd Fd Co RE

Place	Date	Hour	Summary of Events and Information (Ref Map 57 D. 62 D)	Remarks and references to Appendices
V 20 d 6.4	16.5.18		Relieved 518th Fd Coy RE, & took over billets, & work in line from W19 b. to W 1 25 b.	SM
"	17.5.18		No 1-3 & 4 Section work in line. No 2 Section work on accommodation.	SM
"	18.5.18		No 1 & 4 Section wiring front line, No 3 Section accommodation deepening & firestepping Reserve line. No 2 Section making accommodation for Coy at V 20 d 6.4	SM
"	19.5.18		As for 18th	SM
"	20.5.18		As for 18th	SM
"	21.5.18		As for 18th	SM
"	22.5.18		As for 18th	SM
WARLOY U24 c 7.8	23.5.18		Moved to WARLOY U24 c 7.8 relieving 504th Fd Co RE	SM
	24.5.18		Work on Baths & Signal Shelter in WARLOY	SM
	25.5.18		As for 24th	SM
	26.5.18		As for 24th	SM
	27.5.18		As for 24th	SM
	28.5.18		Relieved 511th Fd Co RE in right section [illegible] to Avenue at C 5 b 7.8 [illegible] Sheet (62 D) No 2 + 3 Section to HENNENCOURT [illegible]	SM
C 5 b 7.8	29.5.18		No 2 + 3 Section work in front line No 1 Section Shelter for [illegible] at [illegible]. No 4 Section work on MELBOURNE TRENCH	SM
	30.5.18		As for 29th	SM
	31.5.18		As for 29th except for No 1 Section who worked on Shelter for Coy at C 5 b 7.7. Handing over to 92nd Fd Co RE	SM

S M Chapman Maj
OC 503 Fd Co RE

(A7092) Wt W12839/M1293 75,0 0. 1/17. D. D. & L., Ltd. Forms/C.2118/14.

Vol 18

WAR DIARY

OF

503RD (WESSEX) FIELD COY R.E

FOR PERIOD 1-6-18 TO 30-6-18

VOL XVII

Instructions regarding War Diaries and Intelligence Summaries are contained in F. S. Regs., Part II. and the Staff Manual respectively. Title pages will be prepared in manuscript.

WAR DIARY
or
~~INTELLIGENCE SUMMARY.~~
(Erase heading not required.)

Army Form C. 2118.

503rd Fd Coy RE

Place	Hour, Date	Summary of Events and Information (Ref Map. 57 D, 62 D)	Remarks and references to Appendices
C 6.7.8.	1. 6. 18	Taking over work from 79th Fd Coy RE, Coy working on shelters for DHQ at VADENCOURT	SM
	2. 6. 18	No 1 + 4 Section work on shelters at VADENCOURT. No 2 + 3 resting	SM
	3. 6. 18	No 2 + 3 Section work on BAISIEUX System No 1 + 4 [illegible]	SM
	4. 6. 18	Work for No 2 + 3 Section as for 3rd Nos 1 + 4 resting	SM
	5. 6. 18	Moved from C 6.7.8. to B 9 a 3.3. (62 D) [illegible]	SM
B 9 a. 3.3	~~6. 6. 18~~	Lt E.N. NALL RE, No 504321 Sapr E PALMER mentioned in despatches [illegible] Capt Channing proceeded on leave to UK.	SM
	6. 6. 18	Coy settling into [illegible] Major [illegible] awarded [illegible] [illegible]	SM
	7. 6. 18	Coy packed all stores ready for immediate move after packing Sections training in [illegible] [illegible]	SM
	8. 6. 18	Coy Training.	SM
	9. 6. 18	Church Parade. Ribbons presented to Maj [illegible] Lt E.N. NALL + [illegible] A TUCKER by Corps Commander III Corps [illegible] Following reinforcements reported [illegible] from 7th inst. No 245180 Sapr TAYLOR.N. No 360057 Sapr [illegible] No 414358 Dr ALLEN N.[illegible] No 514122 Dr CATTAN [illegible] No [illegible] Dr BUCHANAN J.	SM
	10. 6. 18	Coy moved by bus to SEUX P 20 c. 7.3. [illegible]	SM
P 20 c. 7.3 (62 D)	11. 6. 18	Settling into billets	SM
	12. 6. 18	Coy training. Repair of [illegible] at SEUX	SM
	13. 6. 18	Coy Training, all sections [illegible] [illegible] [illegible]	SM
	14. 6. 18	Pontooning at DREUIL on the SOMME	SM
	15. 6. 18	Pontooning at DREUIL	SM
	16. 6. 18	Church Parade	SM
	17. 6. 18	Packing ready for move	SM

(73989) W4141—463. 400,000. 9/14. H.&J.Ltd. Forms/C. 2118/10.

Instructions regarding War Diaries and Intelligence Summaries are contained in F. S. Regs., Part II. and the Staff Manual respectively. Title pages will be prepared in manuscript.

WAR DIARY
or
~~INTELLIGENCE SUMMARY.~~
(Erase heading not required.)

503rd Fd Coy RE

Army Form C. 2118.

Hour, Date, Place	Ref Map 57D – 62D Summary of Events and Information	Remarks and references to Appendices
P20c 7 3 (62D)		
C11 d 1.7 18.6.18	Moved by bus to MOLLIENS-AU-BOIS & bivouacked for night	SM
19.6.18	Marched to BOIS ROBERT & took over billets from 517 Coy RE & work of 518 Coy RE. ~~Reconnoitred [illegible] with CRE~~	SM
20.6.18	Settling into billets. ~~[illegible]~~	SM
21.6.18	Laying out & spitlocking new trench on LAVIEVILLE system from D10 a 1.7 to D16 a 6 1. No 4 section working on trench at night. No 2 Section on Adv DHQ at Q14 c 6.2. No 1 work in LAVIEVILLE system with [illegible] Bde. 1438 [illegible] work making frames for shelters. 2nd Lt G. DOYLE RE reported from Base [illegible] ROBERT on 20th inst. Lt D. A. DAVIS reported for duty from 511 Fd Coy RE	SM No 504 [illegible] [illegible] HARRIS RA wounded & evacuated on 20.6.18
22.6.18	No 1 Section work in LAVIEVILLE system. No 2 Sect at DHQ. No 3. Frames for shelters. No 4 [illegible] new trench [illegible] BOIS ROBERT	SM No 504478 [illegible] BAILEY transferred to [illegible] Engineers [illegible]
23.6.18	No 3 Sect work on Bath House at MIRVAUX [illegible] in camp. No 4 Sect Bath at BOIS ROBERT. No work on [illegible] owing to Bde Relief	SM SM (CRE [illegible] No 77)
24.6.18	Test manning of BAZIEUX defence system. No 4 Section work on Bath at BOIS ROBERT. No 504359 Cpl A. TUCKER awarded the MERITORIOUS SERVICE MEDAL (London Gazette dated 3.6.18)	SM
25.6.18	Took over work from 511 Fd Coy RE in Right Section. No 1 Section work on Salvin [illegible] accommodation. No 2 [illegible] making [illegible] in camp. No 3 & 4 Section [illegible] TRENCH also deepening, widening & fire stepping of [illegible]. No 556213 L/Cpl SANDHAM TC & [illegible] joined unit on transfer from 518th Fd Coy RE (Authority CR 1328 T/212 C of 14.6.18). No 524725 Sapr C [illegible] wounded & remained at duty	SM Section E 19 b 5.0 to E 13 d 3.0

(73989) W4141—463. 400,000. 9/14. H.&J.Ltd. Forms/C. 2118/10.

Instructions regarding War Diaries and Intelligence Summaries are contained in F. S. Regs., Part II. and the Staff Manual respectively. Title pages will be prepared in manuscript.

WAR DIARY
~~or~~
~~INTELLIGENCE~~ SUMMARY. 503rd Field Coy RE

(*Erase heading not required.*)

Army Form C. 2118.

Hour, Date, Place		Summary of Events and Information Ref Map 57D 62D	Remarks and references to Appendices
6.11 d 1.7	26.6.18	No 1 Section work on Sap[?]. No 2 Section making [illegible]. No 3 Section wiring DOLLY TRENCH. No 4 Section deepening fire stepping & widening DOLLY TRENCH. No 504534 L/Cpl BELBIN & 388334 [illegible] G GRIFFITHS wounded by bomb	[initials]
	27.6.18	Work as for 26th. No 504155 Sgt W A BISHOP reported as reinforcements from RE Base Depot. No 504628 Sap ARCHDOLEY transferred to [illegible] [illegible] CRE	[initials]
	28.6.18	Work as for 26th inst. Coy HQ & No 2 Section moved to C A 6.4	[initials]
C A 6.4	29.6.18	Work as for 26th inst	[initials]
	30.6.18	Work as for 26th inst	[initials]

S N Chapman Maj
OC 503rd F Coy RE

(73989) W4141—463. 400,000. 9/14. H.&J.Ltd. Forms/C. 2118/10.

Vol 19

War Diary

of

503rd (Wessex) Field Co. R.E.

for Period

1-7-18 to 31-7-18

VOL. XVIII

Instructions regarding War Diaries and Intelligence Summaries are contained in F. S. Regs., Part II. and the Staff Manual respectively. Title pages will be prepared in manuscript.

WAR DIARY
or
~~INTELLIGENCE SUMMARY.~~
(Erase heading not required.)

Army Form C. 2118.

503rd Fd Co RE

Hour, Date, Place	Ref Map SENLIS SHEET 1/20 000 Summary of Events and Information	Remarks and references to Appendices
C 5 a. 6. 4. 1. 7. 18	No 1 Section work on Bn [illegible] in front line [illegible] E 13. b 9.7 & [illegible] C 7. 5. No 2 Section work in Camp. No 3 Section [illegible] ENERGY TRENCH E13 b. & No 4 Section improving [illegible] (E13 a & b).	[illegible]
2. 7. 18	As for 1st inst. Capt [illegible] returned from leave	[illegible]
3. 7. 18	Work as for 1st inst. Capt L. C. [illegible] proceeded to join 490th [illegible] to take command of Coy	[illegible]
4. 7. 18	Work as for 1st inst. Driver Wolfe. A. (504475) transferred to 490 Fld Coy. R.E.	[illegible]
5. 7. 18	No work owing to Coy [illegible] promoted to A/Capt & to be 2nd in Command of Coy	[illegible]
6. 7. 18	Handed over work in [illegible] to 504th [illegible] Took over work from 504th [illegible]	[illegible]
7. 7. 18	No 1 Section work on BAILLEUX SYSTEM. No 2 Section work on [illegible] No 3 Section work on the [illegible] No 4 Section work [illegible] LAVIVILLE [illegible]	[illegible]
8. 7. 18	[illegible] Practice Man Battle Positions received 9.40 pm No night work	[illegible]
9. 7. 18	No 1 Sect handed over work to No 2 Sect and moved to BAVELINCOURT (C14.3) & worked on Right Railway Siding. Other Sections as for 7th. No 526090 Dr Valentine S and No 524344 Dr Herbert A. S. reported as reinforcements from R E B D	[illegible]
10. 7. 18	Work as for 9th	[illegible]
11 7 18	" " " 9th	[illegible]
12. 7. 18	No. 1–2 Sects work as for 9th No night work. Taking over work from 571st Fld Coy RE in left Bde Sector. No 2 on Right Batt Front, No 4 on Left Batt Front. Lt Doyle in Support – No 3 – Batts at D7 b 6.6. No 2 & 4 Sections moved to forward billets at D10. a. 1.5. & handed over to 571st Fld Coy work in rear zone. Major S. W. Chapman M.C proceeded on leave	[illegible]

(73989) W4141—463. 400,000. 9/14. H.&J.Ltd. Forms/C. 2118/10.

Army Form C. 2118.

Instructions regarding War Diaries and Intelligence Summaries are contained in F. S. Regs., Part II. and the Staff Manual respectively. Title pages will be prepared in manuscript.

WAR DIARY

or

~~INTELLIGENCE SUMMARY.~~

(Erase heading not required.)

Page 2

503rd Fld Coy R.E.

Place	Date 1918	Hour	Ref Map SENLIS Sheet 1/20000 Summary of Events and Information	Remarks and references to Appendices
C5a 6.9	July 13th	-	No 1 Sect Work in Camp. No 2 Shelters in front line + improving trenches, No 3 Section Bath at D9b 66 No 4 Wiring Pioneer Tr + Shelters in front line. 2/Lt Doyle wiring SHRINE TR + Shelters in DITTON TR + SHRINE TR	HW
	14th	-	As for 13th except No 4 felling trees on Amiens Albert Road in No Mans Land	HW
	15th	-	As for 13th No 2 took over shelters in SHRINE TR + No 4 shelters in DITTON TR from 2/Lt Doyle	HW
			No 490093 Dr Mair J reported as reinforcement from R.E. B.D.	HW
	16th	-	As for 15th except no wiring party on SHRINE TR.	HW
	17th		As for 15th except 2/Lt Doyle wiring DIGGERS AVENUE	HW
	18		As for 17th No 504017 C.S.M. Hurst proceeded to England for Cadet Course. No 504781 Spr Tanner H.G. reported from 99th Fld Coy R.E. on being transferred from that Coy	HW
	19.		As for 17th 1. Off 14 O.R. 108th Regt U.S. Engineers attached to Coy for instruction	HW
	20		As for 17th except no work in Right Sub sector owing to Gas projection. No work on DIGGERS AV owing to relief	HW
	21.		As for 17th except no work in Line (Parties cancelled by 175 Bgde	HW
	22		As for 14th	HW
	23.		As for 14th	HW
	24		As for 14th / 504525 Cpl Richards E.C. + 504576 Spr Keefe F admitted hospital wounded (Gas)	HW
	25		As for 14th	HW
	26.		Lieut Aldous - No 3 Section as for 14th Handed over work in Left Batt Sector to 520th Fld Coy RE 47th Div + work in right Batt Sector to 311th Fld Coy R.E. No 1 Section moved to BAYELINCOURT C4.b 2.3 and No 2 Section to BEHENCOURT C19 a 55 No 4 Sect returned to Coy HQ.	HW
	27th		Working in conjunction with 504th Fld Coy RE. No 1 Sect Light Rly Siding BAYELINCOURT No 2 Sect Light Rly siding BEHENCOURT No 3 Sect Notice Boards - Expl in wire on DAWIN LAVIEVILLE + BAIZIEUX Systems. No 4 Sect in Camp. Took over work from 504th Fld Coy RE	HW

(A7092). Wt W12839/M1293. 75 ,0.0. 1/17. D. D. & L., Ltd. Forms/C.2118/14.

Instructions regarding War Diaries and Intelligence Summaries are contained in F. S. Regs., Part II. and the Staff Manual respectively. Title pages will be prepared in manuscript.

WAR DIARY

or

~~INTELLIGENCE SUMMARY.~~

(*Erase heading not required.*)

Page 3.

503rd Fld Coy R.E.

Army Form C. 2118.

Place	Date 1918 July	Hour	Summary of Events and Information	Remarks and references to Appendices
C.5.a.6.2	28	-	As yesterday.	[illegible]
	29	-	As for 24th Major S. W. Chapman rejoined Coy from leave	[illegible]
	30	-	As for 24th	[illegible]
	31st	-	Handed over work to 511 Fld Coy R.E. – took over from that Coy in Left Bgde Sector. Nos 1 2 & 3 Sections moved to D.19.c	[illegible]

S.W. Chapman Maj.
O.C. 503rd F.C. R.E.

(A7092). Wt. W12839/M1293 75,0 0. 1/17. D. D. & L., Ltd. Forms/C.2118/14.

58th Divl. Engineers

503rd FIELD COMPANY,

ROYAL ENGINEERS,

A U G U S T   1 9 1 8.

11

Army Form C. 2118.

603rd 7th Co RE

WAR DIARY
or
~~INTELLIGENCE SUMMARY.~~

(Erase heading not required.)

Instructions regarding War Diaries and Intelligence Summaries are contained in F. S. Regs., Part II. and the Staff Manual respectively. Title pages will be prepared in manuscript.

20

Ref Map SENLIS 1/20000 Sheet 62 D.

Place	Date	Hour	Summary of Events and Information	Remarks and references to Appendices
[illegible]	1.8.18		No I Section work on DUKE ST running front line from DOG ST to Right flank. No 2 Section Russian sap & gas proofing dugouts. No 3 Section improvement of DARWIN TRENCH. No 4 Section work in Camp & RE dump BAISIEUX	SM
	2.8.18		As for 1st inst	SM
	3.8.18		Handing over work to 69th Field Coy RE ~~Coy~~ — Coy proceeded by march route to bivouac in BOIS ESCARDONNEUSE I.1.15. a & b Sheet 62 D.	
I 15 a.5.5. 62 D	4.8.18		No 1 Section forming RE dump at BONNAY I.17.c. No 2 Section fitting partitions in Tanks for Tank 18th. No 3 & 4 Section Camp work	SM
	5.8.18		As for 4th inst	SM
	6.8.18		No 2 Section loading tanks with RE material. No 3 Section [illegible] [illegible] forward work [illegible]	SM
	7.8.18		As for 6th except that forward work [illegible]	[illegible]
	8.8.18		Work as for 7th. No 2 & 4 Section moved to valley in K [illegible]	
	9.8.18		No 2 [illegible] [illegible] in K 17. No 3 [illegible] [illegible] No 1 Section [illegible]	
	10.8.18		No 1 3 & 4 Section [illegible] [illegible] No 2 Section [illegible] [illegible]	
	11.8.18		No 1 3 & 4 Section [illegible]	
	12.8.18		No 1 3 [illegible] [illegible]	[illegible]
	13.8.18		No 1 3 [illegible] Section [illegible] No 2 Section work [illegible]	
	14.8.18		[illegible] No [illegible]	

(A7092). Wt W12539/M1293. 75,000. 1/17. D. D. & L., Ltd. Forms/C.2118/14.

Instructions regarding War Diaries and Intelligence Summaries are contained in F. S. Regs., Part II. and the Staff Manual respectively. Title pages will be prepared in manuscript.

WAR DIARY
or
~~INTELLIGENCE~~ SUMMARY.
(Erase heading not required.)

503rd Field Coy R.E.

Army Form C. 2118.

Place	Date	Hour	Summary of Events and Information	Remarks and references to Appendices
			Ref Map sheet 62 D	
I 15 a 5.5. 62 D	15.8.18		Coy Training. No 524280 Dr HARDING R.B. 550643 Sap KEATCH A.G. 545313 Sap COOK W. 398385 Sap COULSON R. reported as reinforcement from R.E. Base Depot	SWC
	16.8.18		Coy Training	SWC
	17.8.18		Coy Training	SWC
	18.8.18		Church Parade	SWC
	19.8.18		Coy Training	SWC
	20.8.18		Coy Sports	SWC
	21.8.18		Coy Training	SWC
	22.8.18		Coy Training	SWC
	23.8.18		Coy Training	SWC
	24.8.18		Moved to J 24 b 0 3. No 4 Section attached to 175th Infantry Brigade	SWC
	25.8.18		Moved to K 16 d 4 2. No 3 Section and party of 1/4 Suffolks (Pioneers) work on forward roads and tracks filling in shell holes &c. Lt Bevis searches for land-mines.	
	26.8.18		Nos 2 & 3 Sects work on Adv. D.H.Q. at L 1 b 3 0 under 2/Lt ALDOUS. Lt BEVIS & 6 OR search for land-mines &c. 10 landmines found and destroyed. 2/Lt ALDOUS rejoined unit from leave in FRANCE. Capt. E. WALL MC rejoined unit from leave to ENGLAND. 470013 CSM CHAPLIN H reported as reinforcement from R.E. Base Depot and taken on strength 25.8.18.	SWC
	27.8.18		No 1 Section erecting water troughs. No 2 Section fixing water tanks. No 3 Sect. work on Adv. D.H.Q. Lieut BEVIS & 6 OR searching for landmines. 1 found and destroyed.	SWC
	28.8.18		Moved to L 1 d 9 8. No 3 Sect. work on Adv. D.H.Q. Lt BEVIS & 7 OR work on shelter at F 28 c 9 2. No 1 Sect improved site at water point.	SWC
	29.8.18		No 3 Sect. work on Adv. D.H.Q. No 4 Sect. joined H.Q. 175th Inf. Bde.	SWC
A 25 d 4 2 (62 C)	30.8.18		Moved to A 25 d 4 2 (62 C). Nos 1, 2 & 3 Sects work on Adv. D.H.Q. at A 19 b 6 2.	SWC
	31.8.18		Nos 1 & 2 Sects dismantling water troughs and water tanks and re-erecting same. No 3 Sect. work on Adv. D.H.Q.	

S W Chapman Maj
OC 503rd Fd Co RE
1/9/18

(A7092). Wt W12839/M1293 75,000. 1/17. D. D. & L., Ltd. Forms/C.2118/14.

14

VR 21

WAR DIARY

of

503rd (WESSEX) FIELD Coy R.E.(T)

FOR PERIOD

1 - 9 - 18 TO 30 - 9 - 18

VOL XIX

Army Form C. 2118.

WAR DIARY
or
INTELLIGENCE SUMMARY.
(*Erase heading not required.*)

Instructions regarding War Diaries and Intelligence Summaries are contained in F. S. Regs., Part II. and the Staff Manual respectively. Title pages will be prepared in manuscript. Ref. Map 62 c. 1/40000.

Place	Date	Hour	Summary of Events and Information	Remarks and references to Appendices
A.25 d.4.2.	1.9.18.		Nos 1 + 3 Sections work on accommodation for 74th D.H.Q. No 2 Section removing pontoons from BONNAY and removing same to K.16 c. BRICKFIELD DUMP. Handing over to 5th R.M.R.E. (74th Divn). No 4 Section returned from 175th Infantry Bde H.Q.	FM
"	2.9.18.		No 1 Section work on accommodation for H.Q. 175th Inf. Bde. Lt WIGHT + 12 O.R. work on wells and erecting baths. Remainder of company collecting salvage.	FM
"	3.9.18.		Nos 2 + 3 Sections work on Adv. D.H.Q. Nos 1 + 4 Sections collect salvage. Lt WIGHT + 12 O.R. work on well + baths at H.3.b. Bombed by E.A. at 9.0 p.m. Killed. 504542 Driver L.J. HUMPHRIES. Wounded and evacuated 504130 Corpl. R.P. PAYNE, 504750 L.Corpl A.J. MILLS, 504463 Sapper H.H. OSBOURNE, 504496 Sapper T.C.Y. SEAGER, 506531 Sapper A.J. WEAVER, 504580 Sapper W.G. OCKWELL. Wounded and remains at duty 504441 Driver RUSSELL E.T. 1 Horse 2 Mules killed. 1 Mule wounded.	FM
	4.9.18.		Moved to B.21 a 5.6. Work completed at adv. D.H.Q. by No 2 Section. Lt WIGHT and 16 O.R. work on well + baths at H.3b. Lt ALDOUS proceeded on Lewis Gun Course at III Corps School.	FM
B.21 a 5.6	5.9.18.		Pontoons collected from BRICKFIELD DUMP and deposited at A.30 a 5.3. Remainder of company not employed on this collected salvage and improved accommodation in camp.	FM
	6.9.18.		Nos 1 Sect moved to Bde. HQ. Nos 2 + 4 Sections collected salvage. No 3 Sect. loaded pontoons and trestles and brought same back to camp. 554066 Dr McGEE W and 494499 Dr Bunn W.J. reported as reinforcement from R.E. Base Depot. Taken on strength from 5th inst. Took over from 517th Field Co. R.E. (47th Divn)	FM
"	7.9.18.		Moved to C.18.c.8.2. Coy worked on water supplies, water + track reconnaissances. 504579 Corpl. G.W.H. FISHER, 504413 Corpl. C BUTLER + 504409 L.Corpl. A.G. WHITTAKER awarded MILITARY MEDALS.	FM
MOISLAINS	8.9.18.		Nos 2 + 4 Sections moved forward to D.18 a 6575. 504321 Sergt. G.G. PALMER mentioned in despatches London GAZETTE MAY 17th 1918. Nos 2 + 4 Sections made water reconnaissances. No 3 Sect. erected horse troughs and worked on water supplies in MOISLAINS.	FM
	9.9.18.		No 4 Sect rejoined H.Q. No 2 Sect. made water reconnaissance. Nos 3 + 4 Sects worked on water supplies in MOISLAINS.	FM
	10.9.18.		No 2 Sect. made reconnaissances for landmines and booby traps. Nos 3 + 4 worked on water supplies in MOISLAINS. Work in MOISLAINS on water supplies handed over (after days work) to 1st Siege Co. R.A.R.E.	FM
	11.9.18.		No 2 Sect. repaired tracks. Nos 3 + 4 Sections worked on accommodation for company at D.18 a 6575. No 4 Sections remained at site. 504539 2nd Corpl HODGES H.F. promoted Corpl. 504530 L.Corpl Dash G.G. promoted 2nd Corpl 504409 A/2nd Corpl. WHITTAKER A.G. appointed L.Corpl. Paid. Lt BILHAM proceeded on leave.	FM
	12.9.18.		Coy moved to D.3.a 5.5. No 3 Sect worked on water supply in MOISLAINS and took pontoons to BOUCHAVESNES. Nos 2 + 4 Sections worked on water supplies, horse standings and tracks in NURLU.	FM

(A7092). Wt W12839/M1293. 750,000. 1/17. D. D. & L., Ltd. Forms/C.2118/14.

Instructions regarding War Diaries and Intelligence Summaries are contained in F. S. Regs., Part II. and the Staff Manual respectively. Title pages will be prepared in manuscript.

WAR DIARY
or
INTELLIGENCE SUMMARY.
(Erase heading not required.)

Army Form C. 2118.

Place	Date	Hour	Summary of Events and Information	Remarks and references to Appendices
NURLU	13.9.18		No 2 + 4 Sections worked on water supplies horse standings and tracks in NURLU. Removing tanks from V.28c73. No 3 worked on water supplies in MOISLAINS.	SNC
	14.9.18		No 2 + 4 Sections worked on horse standings and water supplies in NURLU. No 3 worked on water supplies and horse standings in MOISLAINS.	SNC
	15.9.18		Nos 2 + 3 Secks worked on Horse Trough Standings in MOISLAINS, Baths and paths at D.H.Q. No 4 as yesterday.	SNC
	16.9.18		No 2 Seck worked on Horse Standings in camp and repaired tanks. No 3 Seck completed Horse Standings in MOISLAINS. No 4 Seck as yesterday. II LIEUT C.A.J. BILHAM awarded MILITARY CROSS. (III C.R.O. No. 581.)	SNC
	17.9.18		No 2 Seck as yesterday. No 3 Seck worked under 504th Field Co. R.E. preparing camouflage and splinter proofing pumping Station near HERMONT. No 4 Seck as yesterday. Work in NURLU handed over to 283 A.T. Co. R.E.	SNC
	18.9.18		Nos 2 + 4 Secks filled in shell holes in tracks and fixed Trench bridge near PEIZIERE. No 3 as yesterday	SNC
	19.9.18		~~No~~ Work as yesterday.	SNC
	20.9.18		Nos 2 + 4 Secks worked on tracks and Horse Lines in camp. No 3 Seck on Horse Lines in camp. 408944 Spr CRUST G.F., 304990 Pnr BENNETT J.F. 522773 Dr GOLDING O., 522533 Dr GAMMONS, 534246 2/Cpl. Thunder W.H. reported as reinforcement from R.E. Base Depot and taken on strength.	SNC
	21.9.18		Nos 2 + 3 Secks continued work on horse lines. No 4 Seck reconnoitred tracks and assisted with horse lines. 470377 A/C.S.M. BRAMHALL J reported for duty vice 470013 C.S.M. CHAPLIN J. Transfers between 527th Field Co. R.E. and this unit.	SNC
	22.9.18		Nos 2 + 3 as yesterday. No 4 reconnoitring tracks and collecting salvage.	SNC
	23.9.18		No 4 work on tracks and fixing artillery bridge. Nos 2 + 3 cleaning and packing ready for move. LIEUT. ALDOUS B.C. rejoined from Lewis Gun Course.	SNC
	24.9.18		moved by road to GUILLEMONT T.17.a.7.9. (57c).	SNC

(A7092). Wt. W12839/M1293. 750,000. 1/17. D. D. & L., Ltd. Forms/C.2118/14.

Instructions regarding War Diaries and Intelligence Summaries are contained in F. S. Regs., Part II. and the Staff Manual respectively. Title pages will be prepared in manuscript.

WAR DIARY
or
INTELLIGENCE SUMMARY.
(Erase heading not required.)

Army Form C. 2118.

Place	Date	Hour	Summary of Events and Information	Remarks and references to Appendices
	25.9.18.		Cleaning up and packing ready for move.	
	26.9.18.		Moved by road to DERNACOURT and entrained at 7 30 pm.	
	27.9.18.		Detrained AUBIGNY, and proceeded to CAMBLAIN L'ABBE. D. 22. b 11. (44 B).	
	28.9.18.		Nos 1 & 2 Sect. Company employed. Nos 3 & 4 Sect. worked on accommodation at CAMBLAIN L'ABBE. Lieut G.A.J. BILHAM rejoined from leave.	
	29.9.18.		No. 1 Sect. worked on accommodation. No 3 Sect. moved forward as Advance Party to take over new camp. Nos 2 & 4 Sect. rest.	
	30.9.18.		HQ & No 2, 3 & 4 Section moved [illegible] front from 129th Field Coy RE	

(A7092). Wt W12839/M1293. 750,000. 1/17. D. D. & L., Ltd. Forms/C.2118/14.

6

WAR DIARY
of
503RD FIELD COY R E
FOR PERIOD
1-10-18 TO 31-10-18

VOL XXII

Army Form C. 2118.

WAR DIARY
or
INTELLIGENCE SUMMARY.
(Erase heading not required.)

Instructions regarding War Diaries and Intelligence Summaries are contained in F. S. Regs., Part II. and the Staff Manual respectively. Title pages will be prepared in manuscript. Mobile 44 Bde 44A + 44

Vol 22

Place	Date	Hour	Summary of Events and Information	Remarks and references to Appendices
ABLAIN-St-NAZIARE	1.10.18		Nos 1 + 4 Sections made petrol tin piers, frames etc. in camp making and painting notice boards. No 2 Sect clearing road and filling shell holes in LENS - LIEVIN Road. No 3 Sect worked on this road digging gutters &c. Major S W Chapman MC proceeded on leave in France	SW
	2.10.18		No. 1 Sect. worked on petrol tin piers &c. Remainder worked on clearing & repairing LENS - LIEVIN Rd.	SW
	3.10.18		No 1 Sect att 175th Infantry Bde. No. 2 Sect. clearing fallen girder bridge. No 3 Sect. worked on water points &c. No 4 Sect. on petrol tin pier in camp.	SW
	4.10.18		No 1 As yesterday. No 2 as yesterday. No 3 clearing fallen bridge. No 4 clearing & repairing road in LENS.	SW
ANGRES	5.10.18		HQ moved to M.33.a.15. Nos 2 & 3 moved to LIEVIN. No 4 & 1 Sect. cleared road in LENS. No 2 & 3 clearing fallen bridge.	SW
	6.10.18		No 1 2 + 4 Sections. Work as for yesterday. No 3 Section constructing Adv DHQ at BULLY	SW
	7.10.18		as for yesterday. Nos 1 2 + 3 Sections. No 4 Section work on billets at St PIERRE	SW
	8.10.18		No 1 Section moved to M6 a 7 2. Work on accommodation for Bde HQrs. Nos 2 + 3 Sections moved to CITE ST PIERRE (M11 central). No 3 Section work as for yesterday. No 2 Section clearing tunnels digging + widening CT at H34 & 6 3. Relieved 511th Field Coy RE in Left Brigade Front night 8/9th	SW
CITE St PIERRE	9.10.18		HQrs moved to CITE ST PIERRE. Nos 2 + 3 sections work on roads forward. No 1 same as yesterday. No 4 accommodation for forward billets	SW

(A7092) Wt W12839/M1293 75,000 1/17. D. D. & L., Ltd. Forms/C.2118/14.

Instructions regarding War Diaries and Intelligence Summaries are contained in F. S. Regs., Part II. and the Staff Manual respectively. Title pages will be prepared in manuscript.

WAR DIARY
or
INTELLIGENCE SUMMARY.
(Erase heading not required.)

Army Form C. 2118.

Sheet 44B 44A 44 [partly illegible]

Sheet 2.

Hour, Date, Place		Summary of Events and Information	Remarks and references to Appendices
10/10/18	CITE ST PIERRE	work as for yesterday. Major S W Chapman MC returns from leave	[initials]
11/10/18	do	No 3 Section work on Forward Roads. No 1 Section constructing Bde HQrs + gas blanketing dugouts + clearing well. No 2 Improvement of billets. No 4 making marsh mats	SM
12/10/18	do	No 1 same as yesterday. 3 preparing forward Bde HQrs + work on forward Roads. No 2 clearing + searching dugouts. No 4 + Transport Lines moved to CITÈ ST PIERRE	SM
13-10 18	do.	Work same as yesterday for No 3 Section. No 2+4 work on LENS-CARVIN Rd. No 1 Section moved to CITE ST AUGUSTE. No 504389 Dr MILLS R G reinforcement from 247 Fd Coy	SM
14.10 18	CITE du GRAND CONDE	HQrs Horse Lines + No 4 Section + No 3 Section moved to CITE du GRAND CONDE. No 1 Section + 2 Section moved to FOSSE 9. No 1+2 Section repairing bridge at O8c74	SM
15 10 18	do	No 3 Section moved to FOSSE 9. Constructing advanced DHQ. No 4 Section repairing roads. No 1 Section Bridge at O8c75 opened for HT. No 2 Section searching for Booby traps	SM
16 10 18	COURRIERES.	HQrs No 1 2 3 + 4 Sections moved to COURRIERES. Horse lines at MONTIGNY. Works No 1 + 3 Sections works as for yesterday. No 2 Section erecting footbridge for Infantry across CANAL de la HAUTE DEULE + clearing debris for Bridge at P1 b 8.5. Section attached to Brigade. No 4 Section clearing bridge sites. No 3 + 4 sections erecting bridge at [illegible] P1 a 4.5	SM
17 10 18	do	Works. No 1 Section Filling crater + opening road at I33 b 3.3. No 3 Section + 4 Section medium pontoon bridge across CANAL de la HAUTE DEULE at P2 a 1.2. No 2 Section clearing road round crater at P6 a 85 20. Moved with advanced Brigade	SM
18 10 18	FAUMONT	HQrs Nos 1 3 + 4 Section + Horse Lines moved to FAUMONT. No 2 Section moved with advanced Brigade HQrs. Works as necessary on roads. 2Lt BALDOUS leave to U Kingdom	SM
19 10 18	LA PLANQUE	HQrs No 1 3 4 Sections + Horse Lines moved to LA PLANQUE. Sections employed on repairs to roads destroyed by enemy. Crater at G2 d 0150 filled in. Destroyed Culvert at G15 b 0 4 repaired. Crater G16 central filled in also at G16 b 5.6. Culvert at L26 d 73 repaired for double way traffic. Crater at L33 b 0 3 filled in.	SM

(73989) W4141—463. 400,000. 9/14. H.&J.Ltd. Forms/C. 2118/10.

Instructions regarding War Diaries and Intelligence Summaries are contained in F. S. Regs., Part II. and the Staff Manual respectively. Title pages will be prepared in manuscript. Sheet 44B 44A 44

WAR DIARY
or
INTELLIGENCE SUMMARY.
(*Erase heading not required.*)

Sheet 3

Army Form C. 2118.

Place	Date	Hour	Summary of Events and Information	Remarks and references to Appendices
20/10/18 AIX	20/10/18		HQrs Nos 1 3 + 4 Sections + HQrs moved to AIX. No 2 Section moved with advanced Brigade HQrs. Work - Deviation round craters at H9c93 H17a88 H10b15 + G16b58 H17a98. Heavy bridge constructed over destroyed culvert at G11c central	
21/10/18 RUMEGIES	21/10/18		HQrs Nos 1 3 + 4 Section + Horse Lines moved to RUMEGIES. No 2 moved with advance Brigade. Work: Improving deviation at H17a98. Bridge + causeway erected at I9d91. Felling timber for work on craters at I9b3.4. Lt Dakers returned from leave to UK	
22/10/18 do	22/10/18		No 3 Section strengthening bridge at I9d91. No 477105 Spr Rawlinson A joined as reinforcement	
do	23/10/18		Nos 1+3 Sections collecting material for Bridges from TEMPLEUVE	
do	24/10/18		Nos 1+3 Sections sawing timber for bridges. No 4 Section repairing pump + erecting same for bath house. Major C.A.T. CHAPMAN granted 10 days special leave to UK 26/10/18 to 9-11-18	
do	25/10/18		Work same as for yesterday	
do	26/10/18		Work - No 2 Section floating bridge put across CANAL at J3c40. No 1 3 + 4 same as yesterday	
do	27/10/18		Work: No 1 Section filling in craters + repairing road at MAULDE. No 2 Section moved from RONSY to RUMEGIES. 174th Brigade relieved 175th Bde in front Line. Work handed over to 511th Field Coy + taken over their work in hand. No 444573 Spr Gray W reported from Base as reinforcement	
do	28/10/18		No 4 Section making roadway of Bridges + approaches good at I17b23 H2a79 H3a55. Bridge at H6c81 deviation being conducted by No 2 Section	
	29/10/18		No 4 Section + No 2 Section work as for yesterday. No 1 Section unloading heavy bridging material at MAULDE	
	30/10/18		Work as for yesterday. 12 OR of batt of 175th Batt being instructed in construction of light foot bridges	
	31/10/18		No 4 Section work as for yesterday	
	1/11/18		[signature] Capt for Major, Commanding 503rd (Wessex) Fd. Coy. R.E.	

(A7092). Wt. W12839/M1293. 750,000. 1/17. D. D. & L., Ltd. Forms/C.2118/14.

Instructions regarding War Diaries and Intelligence Summaries are contained in F. S. Regs., Part II. and the Staff Manual respectively. Title pages will be prepared in manuscript. Ref maps 44 + 45

WAR DIARY
or
~~INTELLIGENCE~~ SUMMARY.
(Erase heading not required.)

Army Form C. 2118.

Vol 23

Place	Date	Hour	Summary of Events and Information	Remarks and references to Appendices
RUMEGIES	1.11.18	—	Kit Inspection. No 4 Section patrolling bridges and making roadways up over same	JW
Do.	2.11.18.	—	No 1 Sect. Work on roads at H.16.c. No 3 Sect. Erecting Spray Bath. : No 4 as yesterday.	JW
Do.	3.11.18	—	Nos 2 + 3 Sects. making barrel rafts and piers etc. : No 4 Sect. as yesterday.	JW
Do.	4.11.18	–	No. 3 Sect. as yesterday : No 4 Sect. patrolling roads &c. Making raft and testing same.	JW
Do.	5.11.18.	–	Lieut. D.A. BEVIS proceeded to ROUEN for Course of R.C. Instruction. No 2 Sect. making rafts for Brigade Practice. No 4 Sect. patrolling roads &c.	JW
Do.	6.11.18	–	No 4 Sect. as yesterday.	JW
Do.	7.11.18	–	No 1 Sect. work on roads: No 2 Sect. work on roads and making rifle rests: No 3 Sect. Preparing rafts. No 4 Sect. as yesterday.	JW
Do.	8.11.18	–	Trestle bridge erected at J.3.c.4.0. Pontoon Bridge erected at J.9.b.4.7. Approaches improved. Roads and bridges patrolled as yesterday. Nos 2, 3 + 4 Sects. moved to MAULDE.	JW
Do.	9.11.18.	/	Roads and bridges reconnoitred and made passable where required. : No 3 Sect. moved to PERUWELZ. Remainder of Company to WEIRS. The following reported as reinforcements from R.E. Base Depot. 93122 Spr MURRAY R., 504489 Spr TANNER H.G. 136578 Pnr MARTIN C., 461536 Spr PEARSON J. : 2/Lieut. B.C. ALDOUS rejoined Coy from leave. Lieut. G. DOYLE proceeded on leave to U.K.	JW
WEIRS	10.11.18.	/	Bridge built for Horse Transport at H.1.a.3.5. : Nos 3 + 4 Sects moved to NEUF MAISON. Remainder of Coy to ECHCHERIES.	JW
ECACHERIES.	11.11.18.	/	Hostilities cease at 11.00 hours. Trumpeter HULL sounds "Cease Fire"	JW
Do.	12.11.18	/	Standing by.	
Do	13.11.18	/	Clean Arms and Medical Inspection. Physical training and games.	
Do.	14.11.18	/	Company moved to BELOEIL (B.3.a.6.7. Sheet 45). Major S.W. CHAPMAN M.C. rejoined from leave.	JW

(A7092). Wt W12839/M1293 75,000 1/17. D. D. & L., Ltd. Forms/C.2118/14.

Instructions regarding War Diaries and Intelligence Summaries are contained in F. S. Regs., Part II. and the Staff Manual respectively. Title pages will be prepared in manuscript.

Army Form C. 2118.

WAR DIARY
or
INTELLIGENCE SUMMARY.

(Erase heading not required.)

Place	Date	Hour	Summary of Events and Information	Remarks and references to Appendices
BELOEIL	15.11.18	–	Nos 1 + 2 Secks repairing roads and filling craters. Nos. 3 + 4 Secks cleaning up.	[illegible]
Do.	16.11.18	–	Nos 3 + 4 Secks on works. Nos 1 + 2 Secks. cleaning up. 26777 Sapper CRAWFORD J proceeded to P.G. Base Depot for Medical Board.	[illegible]
Do.	17.11.18	–	Church Parade.	[illegible]
Do.	18.11.18	–	No 1 Seck in camp. No 2 + 3 Secks. work on trestle bridge at ECACHERIES. No 4 Seck work on crater at NEUFMAISON. Bridging equipment fetched from Espain	[illegible]
Do.	19.11.18	–	Work on bridge at ECACHERIES.	[illegible]
Do.	20.11.18	–	Nos 1 + 4 Secks Training. Nos 2 + 3 Secks work on bridge at ECACHERIES.	[illegible]
Do.	21.11.18	–	As yesterday.	[illegible]
Do.	22.11.18	–	Coy. Training.	[illegible]
Do.	23.11.18	–	Coy. Training.	[illegible]
Do.	24.11.18	–	Church Parade.	[illegible]
Do.	25.11.18	–	Coy Training.	[illegible]
Do.	26.11.18	–	As yesterday	[illegible]
Do.	27.11.18	–	As yesterday.	[illegible]
Do.	28.11.18	–	Packing up ready for move. Lieut. G. Dome rejoined from leave.	[illegible]
Do.	29.11.18	–	Moved to WEIRS. (K.4.a.5.5. Sheet 44)	[illegible]
WEIRS	30.11.18	–	Settling in.	[illegible]

(A7092). Wt W12839/M1293. 75,0.0. 1/17. D. D. & L., Ltd. Forms/C.2118/14.

6

W A R   D I A R Y

of

503rd Field Company R.E.

for the period

1.11.18 to 30.11.18.

9

58

Army Form C. 2118.

WAR DIARY
or
INTELLIGENCE SUMMARY.

(Erase heading not required.)

503rd Fd Co R.E.

WO 95/24

Instructions regarding War Diaries and Intelligence Summaries are contained in F. S. Regs., Part II. and the Staff Manual respectively. Title pages will be prepared in manuscript. Ref Sheet 44 1/40,000.

Place	Date	Hour	Summary of Events and Information	Remarks and references to Appendices
WIERS	1.12.18	–	Church Parade	SMC
Do.	2.12.18	–	Nos 1.3 + 4 Secks improving accommodation. No 2 Sect moved to MAULDE to build bridge at MORTAGNE. Educational classes commenced.	SMC
Do.	3.12.18	–	Work as yesterday.	SMC
Do.	4.12.18	–	As yesterday	SMC
Do.	5.12.18	–	No 1 Sect work on baths at PERUWELZ. No 2 Sect rejoined Coy HQ's 25 OR attended Kings Inspection of Division at PERUWELZ. Remainder of Coy worked on accommodation.	SMC
Do.	6.12.18	–	Work on accommodation &c.	SMC
Do.	7.12.18	–	as yesterday	SMC
Do.	8.12.18	–	Church Parade.	SMC
Do.	9.12.18	–	Work as for 7th.	SMC
Do	10.12.18	–	No 4 Sect moved to MAULDE to prepare workshops. Remained of Coy as yesterday.	SMC
Do	11.12.18	–	Work as yesterday	SMC
Do.	12.12.18	–	Work as yesterday. 242139 Spr Watson J.W. 540790 Spr Oates C. reported as reinforcement from R.E. Base Depot.	SMC
Do	13.12.18	–	Work as yesterday.	SMC
Do.	14.12.18	–	Work as yesterday. Lieut. D.A. Bevis returned from Course of instruction. 422030 Spr Clark W. 319347 Spr. Kelly H.C, 391852 Spr. Pendrell T.L. 391340 Spr. Bowie A. 353009 Pnr Cavill A. 476357 Dr Lavelle, 502628 Dvr Grace J. 163050 Dvr Johnson S. 64356 Dvr McCullock S. reported as reinforcement from R.E. Base Depot.	SMC

(A7092). Wt W12839/M1293 75,000 1/17. D. D. & L., Ltd. Forms/C.2118/14.

Instructions regarding War Diaries and Intelligence Summaries are contained in F. S. Regs., Part II. and the Staff Manual respectively. Title pages will be prepared in manuscript.

WAR DIARY
or
INTELLIGENCE SUMMARY.
(Erase heading not required.)

Army Form C. 2118.

503rd Fd Co R.E.

Place	Date	Hour	Summary of Events and Information	Remarks and references to Appendices
WIERS.	15.12.18	—	Church Parade.	SWL
"	16.12.18	—	Nos 1 & 3 Secks as for 14th inst. No 2 Sect work on Footbridge at F 20. a 3 6.	SWL
"	17.12.18	-	As yesterday.	SWL
"	18.12.18	-	As yesterday. 452504 LCpl Ave H, 317678 Spr Murphy T, 504494 Spr Read W, 514889 Spr Dennis G, 504493 Spr Regan W.J, 504335 Spr King H.V. 23878 Spr Morrison T, 108425 Spr Hunter H. rejoined unit from R.E. Base Depot. 18599 L/Cpl Colman F, 554287 Spr Munday H. 336162 Spr Greenfield W.J. 345799 Spr Waine F.E. 352926 Pnr Ward T.H, 370881 Dr Baker C.W. 370581 Dr Wicks A.E.J. 370889 Dr Blake R. 370590 Dr Gass S. 370592 Dr Dyer J.H. 370597 Dr Thacker E. reported as reinforcement from R.E. Base Depot.	SWL
"	19.12.18	-	Work as yesterday.	SWL
"	20.12.18	-	All sections work on accommodation &c.	SWL
"	21.12.18	-	As yesterday	SWL
"	22.12.18	-	Church Parade.	SWL
"	23.12.18	-	As for 21st inst.	SWL
"	24.12.18	-	As yesterday. No 4 Sect rejoined Unit from MAULDE.	SWL
"	25.12.18	"	CHURCH PARADE.	SWL
"	26.12.18	"	NIL.	SWL
"	27.12.18	-	Work as for 24th inst.	SWL
"	28.12.18	"	As yesterday. No 3 Section moved to MAULDE.	SWL
"	29.12.18	-	Church Parade.	SWL
"	30.12.18	-	Work as for 28th inst. 1 Sergt. 15 O.R. moved to LEUZE for work on accommodation for 178th Infantry Brigade.	SWL
"	31.12.18	-	Work As yesterday.	SWL

S. M... [signature] Commanding 503rd (Wessex) Fd Coy R.E.

(A7092). Wt. W12839/M1293 75,0.0. 1/17. D. D. & L., Ltd. Forms/C.2118/14.

14

503 3d Cav Rg

1825

58Aw

WAR DIARY
or
INTELLIGENCE SUMMARY.
(*Erase heading not required.*)

Army Form C. 2118.

Instructions regarding War Diaries and Intelligence Summaries are contained in F. S. Regs., Part II. and the Staff Manual respectively. Title pages will be prepared in manuscript. Ref Map Sheet 44 1/40,000.

Place	Date	Hour	Summary of Events and Information	Remarks and references to Appendices
WIERS	1.1.19.		No 3 Sect. work at MAULDE preparing workshops. 1 NCO & 15 OR work at LEUZE on accommodation of 175th Infantry Bde. Remainder of Coy on accommodation at WIERS.	[initials]
do.	2.1.19		Work as yesterday. 11 Lieut G.W. WIGHT granted leave to U.K. 5-19.1.19.	[initials]
do.	3.1.19		Work as yesterday. 504404 Dr. BRANT F.J proceeded to England for to be demobilized.	[initials]
do	4.1.19		Work as yesterday. 64356 Dr McCORMICK A proceeded to England to be demobilized. Major S.W. CHAPMAN. M.C. proceeded to Officers Rest House.	[initials]
do.	5.1.19		Church Parade. 430097 Spr. GILBERT J. 145724 Spr. VICKERS F proceeded to England to be demobilized	[initials]
do	6.1.19		Work on Baths at WIERS and accommodation. 93460 Spr. DAVIDSON M proceeded to England to be demobilized.	[initials]
do	7.1.19		Work as yesterday.	[initials]
do.	8.1.19.		As yesterday.	[initials]
do	9.1.19.		As yesterday.	[initials]
do	10.1.19		As yesterday.	[initials]
do.	11.1.19.		No 1 Sect details (16 OR) rejoined Co from LEUZE. Remainder of Co work as yesterday.	[initials]
do	12.1.19.		Church Parade. 504185 Dr. Burge H & 398405 Spr. Partridge W proceeded to England for Demobilisation	[initials]

(A7092). Wt W12839/M1293. 75,0,0. 1/17. D. D. & L., Ltd. Forms/C.2118/14.

Instructions regarding War Diaries and Intelligence Summaries are contained in F. S. Regs., Part II. and the Staff Manual respectively. Title pages will be prepared in manuscript.

WAR DIARY
or
INTELLIGENCE SUMMARY.
(Erase heading not required.)

Army Form C. 2118.

Place	Date	Hour	Summary of Events and Information	Remarks and references to Appendices
WIERS.	13.1.19	—	No 3 Sect. at MAULDE. Remainder Cos. work on Bath accommodation at WIERS. 57196 2nd Cpl. Darley E. 403644 Spr. Davidson G. proceeded to England for Demob.	RW.
do.	14.1.19	—	Work as yesterday.	RW.
do.	15.1.19	—	As yesterday.	RW.
do.	16.1.19	—	As yesterday.	RW.
do.	17.1.19	-	As yesterday.	RW.
do	18.1.19	-	As yesterday.	RW.
do	19.1.19	—	Church Parade. 504325 Sgt. Gardner J.S. awarded DCM, 504291 L. Sgt. Yagg A.E. Mentioned in Dispatches } New Years Honours Dispatch 1918 1919.	RW
do	20.1.19	-	Work as Saturday 18th inst. 554006 Sgt. Lipple W.? 504291 Sgt. Yagg A.E. 504583 Spr. Cook F.G.A. 504537 Spr. Burden J. 504410 Spr. Rutter W.G. 504471 Spr. Bishop E. 504626 Spr. Goram H.J. 504444 Spr. Scott H.J. 398081 2nd Corpl. Howell W. 504192 Spr. Grogan W. 481172 Spr. Davies L. 108425 Spr. Hunter H. 88704 Dr. Fraser A.L. proceeded to England for Demobilisation.	RW
do	21.1.19	-	Work as yesterday. 488944 Spr. Emest proceeded to England to be demobilised	RW
do	22.1.19	-	Work as yesterday	RW
do.	23.1.19	-	Work as yesterday	

(A7092). Wt. W12839/M1293. 750,000. 1/17. D. D. & L., Ltd. Forms/C.2118/14.

Army Form C. 2118.

Instructions regarding War Diaries and Intelligence Summaries are contained in F. S. Regs., Part II. and the Staff Manual respectively. Title pages will be prepared in manuscript.

WAR DIARY
or
INTELLIGENCE SUMMARY.

(Erase heading not required.)

Place	Date	Hour	Summary of Events and Information	Remarks and references to Appendices
WIERS.	24.1.19.	–	No 3 Sect. work at MAULDE. Remainder of Co work on accommodation.	DAB
do	25.1.19	–	Work as yesterday. 504300 Sergt Cole G, 477504 L/Cpl Rae H, 417794 Spr. Brown W.K., 187282 Spr. Innes, W.J. 370590 Dr. Gass S. proceeded to England for Demobilisation.	DAB
do	26.1.19	–	Church Parade. Capt. Ewart MC, 504080 Sgt Cross W.G. 504579 Cpl Fisher G.W.H. 504530 2nd Cpl Dash G.G. 504552 L/Cpl Phillips J. 504533 L/Cpl Green A 185874 Spr. Walker T.W. 81900 Spr. Shaw J.T. 495093 Spr. Foster G.J. 504531 Spr. Cadmore R.W. 504593 Spr. Regan W.J. 550043 Spr. Keatch A.J. 6708 Spr. Thompson H. 207883 Spr. Bolton H. 496409 Dr. Wells S. 490449 Dr. Ball W.J. 504094 Dr. Blackmore F.J. 91009 Dr. Freeman T.W. 546140 Dr. Stevens A. 504056 Dr. Hull G.J. 504328 Dr. Stenner A.G. proceeded to England for Demobilisation.	DAB
do	27.1.19.		Work as Saturday. 180213 Spr. Biddle F proceeded to England for Demobilisation.	DAB
do.	28.1.19		Work as yesterday.	DAB

(A7092). Wt W12839/M1293. 750,000. 1/17. D. D. & L., Ltd. Forms/C.2118/14.

Instructions regarding War Diaries and Intelligence Summaries are contained in F. S. Regs., Part II. and the Staff Manual respectively. Title pages will be prepared in manuscript.

WAR DIARY
or
INTELLIGENCE SUMMARY.
(Erase heading not required.)

Army Form C. 2118.

Place	Date	Hour	Summary of Events and Information	Remarks and references to Appendices
WIERS	29.1.19		Work as yesterday. 459691 L/Cpl. Lindsay [illegible]. 504[illegible] L/Cpl. Jones [illegible]. 477104 L/Cpl. Fealks R.H. 504306 L/Cpl. Hale J. 316624 Spr. Vaughan R. 108770 Spr. Taylor A.B., 167228 Spr. Hoult C. 99309 Spr. Pacey S. 370551 Dr. Baker C. 504[illegible] Dr. Edmunds D.C. 504389 2/Cpl. Mack H.J. 506110 Spr. Foster A.W. 144667 Spr. Garrett W. proceeded to England for demobilisation.	[initials]
"	30.1.19		Work as yesterday.	[initials]
"	31.1.19		Work as yesterday.	[initials]

31.1.19.

H. A. Bevis
Lieut. for Major,
Commanding 503rd (Wessex) Fd. Coy. R.E.

7

WAR DIARY
or
INTELLIGENCE SUMMARY.
(Erase heading not required.)

503 Fd Coy RE
58 DW
VR 26

Army Form C. 2118.

Instructions regarding War Diaries and Intelligence Summaries are contained in F. S. Regs., Part II. and the Staff Manual respectively. Title pages will be prepared in manuscript.

Ref Map Sheet 44 1/40000

Place	Date	Hour	Summary of Events and Information	Remarks and references to Appendices
WIERS	1-2-19		Work on accommodation. 470377 CSM Bramhall WJ 398456 Sapr Gair J., 232015 Sapr Green FW 434289 Sapr Johnson W proceeded to England for demobilization	HLH
do	2-2-19		Church Parade 428642 Sapr Marsh A 472108 Sapr Rawlinson A 230773 Sapr Mayfer HG 398385 Sapr Anlsom R 50628 Dvr Grace J 504155 Sergt Bishop WH 471436 Sapr Mohab J 461536 Sapr Pearson J 48782 Sapr Sweetman W 352926 Pnr Ward TH 471387 Sapr Atkinson LJ 504574 2/Cpl Whale HG 504538 Sapr Clark EE 504461 Sapr Hobbs H 504584 Sapr Wheeler A 504508 Sapr Waller S 504534 Sergt Crook HJ 212082 Sapr Butler WH 518783 Sapr Walker W 504529 Corpl Hodges H 504597 Sapr Seller RH 504476 Sapr Crook F 504374 L/Cpl Steer PW 514967 Sapr Back EJ 84373 Corpl Crow H 504165 Sapr Harwood S 277820 Sapr Fisher H 199411 Dvr Hallybone A 534653 L/Cpl Payne EJ 504422 Dvr Rumming S 504433 Sapr Horwood AR 504493 Dvr Wyatt HJ 536099 Dvr Valentine S 504581 Sapr Jones HM 504473 Sapr Cowley W 504334 Sapr Parsons RJ, 2/Lieut BC Aldous, proceeded to UK for demobilization	HLH
do	3-2-19		Work as Saturday 176989 Sapr Pearson JH 360051 Sapr Winstanley J 242139 Sapr Watson JW proceeded to UK for demobilization, Major SW Chapman returned from Rest Home, Nice	HLH
do	4-2-19		Work as yesterday Major SW Chapman & Lieut G Doyle transferred to DADGRYE	HLH
do	5-2-19		Work as yesterday	HLH
do	6-2-19		Work as yesterday 430368 Sapr Hartley W proceeded to UK for demobilization, 504455 Sapr Horsey HH, transferred with Major SW Chapman, to DADGRYE	HLH
do	7-2-19		Work as yesterday Lieut DA Bevis, 89578 Sapr Beeny DR, 245180 Sapr Taylor W proceeded to UK for demobilization	HLH
do	8-2-19		Work as yesterday	HLH
do	9-2-19		Church Parade 504321 Sergt Palmer EJ, 504448 Corpl Johnson WH 504500 L/Cpl Whale EJ 504573 Sapr Butcher L 504522 Sapr Linton EA proceeded to UK for demobilization	HLH

(A7092). Wt W12839/M1293. 750,000. 1/17. D. D. & L., Ltd. Forms/C.2118/14.

Army Form C. 2118.

WAR DIARY
or
INTELLIGENCE SUMMARY.
(Erase heading not required.)

Instructions regarding War Diaries and Intelligence Summaries are contained in F. S. Regs., Part II. and the Staff Manual respectively. Title pages will be prepared in manuscript.

Place	Date	Hour	Summary of Events and Information	Remarks and references to Appendices
WIERS	10-2-19		Work as Saturday. 504453 Sapr Bloom F.C., 504578 Sapr Bruce W, 504494 Sapr Reed W, 504437 Sapr Riches W.J, 504484 Sapr Tanner H.G, 504400 Sapr Jones S.J, 83797 Sapr Bannister J.R, 476776 Sapr Bingham W.R, 476148 Sapr Gosling H, 388334 Sapr Griffiths G, 504563 Cpl Sowen J.B proceeded to UK for demobilization	HH
do	11-2-19		Work as yesterday	HH
do	12-2-19		Work as yesterday	HH
do	13-2-19		Work as yesterday	HH
do	14-2-19		Work as yesterday	HH
do	15-2-19		Work as yesterday	HH
do	16-2-19		Church Parade, 2/Lieut G.W. Wright, demobilized while on leave 19-1-19. 18599 L/Cpl Colman F.V. proceeded to UK for demobilization.	HH
do	17-2-19		Work as Saturday. Detachment rejoined from MAULDE	HH
do	18-2-19		Work as yesterday	HH
do	19-2-19		Work as yesterday. 11 O.R. proceeded to LEUZE for work on Divisional Stores attached to 175th Inf Bde. 216396 Sapr Parsons J.G. proceeded to UK for demobilization	HH
do	20-2-19		Work as yesterday.	HH
do	21-2-19		Work as yesterday + loading vehicles for move	HH
LEUZE	22-2-19		Coy moved from WIERS to LEUZE. Work on accommodation	HH
do	23-2-19		No Church Parade. Work on accommodation	HH

(A7092). Wt W12839/M1293 75 ,0 0 1/17. D. D. & L., Ltd. Forms/C.2118/14.

Army Form C. 2118.

WAR DIARY
or
INTELLIGENCE SUMMARY.

(Erase heading not required.)

Instructions regarding War Diaries and Intelligence Summaries are contained in F. S. Regs., Part II. and the Staff Manual respectively. Title pages will be prepared in manuscript.

Place	Date	Hour	Summary of Events and Information	Remarks and references to Appendices
LEUZE	24-2-19		5 O.R. work under Lieut Wills, remainder on accommodation	HLB
do	25-2-19		4 O.R. work under Lieut Wills remainder on accommodation	HLB
do	26-2-19		4 OR work under Lieut Wills remainder on accommodation	HLB
do	27-2-19		5 OR work under Lieut Wills, remainder on accommodation. Capt H. L. Bazalgette assumed command of Coy	HLB
do	28-2-19		Work on accommodation 2/Lieut J.L. Lishman posted from 504 Field Co RE	HLB

H. L. Bazalgette Capt

Commanding [illegible] R.E

(A7092). Wt W12839/M1293. 75 ,0.0. 1/17. D. D. & L., Ltd. Forms/C.2118/14.

Army Form C. 2118.

WAR DIARY
or
INTELLIGENCE SUMMARY.

(Erase heading not required.)

15 503rd Field Coy R.E.

Instructions regarding War Diaries and Intelligence Summaries are contained in F. S. Regs., Part II. and the Staff Manual respectively. Title pages will be prepared in manuscript. Ref Map Sheet 44 1/40000

Place	Date	Hour	Summary of Events and Information	Remarks and references to Appendices
LEUZE	1-3-19		Work on accommodation	HLB
do	2-3-19		Church Parade. Inspection of transport lines & billets by CRE	HLB
do	3-3-19		5 OR work under Lieut Wells. remainder on accommodation	HLB
do	4-3-19		Work as yesterday	HLB
do	5-3-19		Work as yesterday	HLB
do	6-3-19		Work as yesterday. 556393 LCpl McDiarmid D 319347 Spr Kelly HC 319352 Spr Pendrell TE 342799 Spr Warne FE 304990 Pnr Bennett J 353099 Pnr Carroll A 412707 Driver Hunter A proceeded to join 23rd Field Coy RE	HLB
			H L Bazalgette Capt OC 503rd Field Coy RE	
LEUZE	7-3-19		Work as yesterday. Capt H L Bazalgette admitted to Hospital.	E.B.
do	8-3-19		Work on accommodation 388840 2nd Cpl Fletcher AJ 217696 Sapper Murphy J 506682 Sapper Roberts AS 490348 Sapper Smith R 506539 Sapper Sutton FJ 412670 Driver Buchanan J transferred to 23rd Field Co RE	E.B.
do	9-3-19		Church Parade	E.B.

E. Bulham Lt
a/OC 503rd Field Coy R.E.

(A7092). Wt W12839/M1293. 75,0,0. 1/17. D. D. & L., Ltd. Forms/C.2118/14.

Army Form C. 2118.

Instructions regarding War Diaries and Intelligence Summaries are contained in F. S. Regs., Part II. and the Staff Manual respectively. Title pages will be prepared in manuscript.

WAR DIARY
or
INTELLIGENCE SUMMARY.
(*Erase heading not required.*)

503rd Field Coy R.E.

Place	Date	Hour	Summary of Events and Information	Remarks and references to Appendices
LEUZE	10-3-19		5. O.R work under Lieut Wills, remainder on accommodation	E.B.
do	11-3-19		Re-arranging wagon park, improving billets	E.B.
do	12-3-19		Work as yesterday	E.B.
do	13-3-19		Checking Tool Carts and Bridging Equipment. Improving billets	E.B.
do	14-3-19		Arranging Concert Hall for R.E. Band, Improving billets	E.B.
do	15-3-19		Bathing Parade. Cleaning Concert Hall	E.B.
do	16-3-19		Church Parade. 370597 Driver Thaxter E. proceeded to UK for demobilization	E.B.
do	17-3-19		Checking Tool Carts & bridging equipment. Improving billets. Transfer of the following NCO & men to 23rd Field Co. R.E. is cancelled. 388600 2/Cpl Fletcher A.J. 217676 Sapper Murphy J. 490348 Sapper Smith B. 506539 Sapper Sutton D.J. 504682 Sapper Rodda A.S. 412610 Driver Buchanan J.	E.B.
do	18-3-19		Checking Tool Carts & bridging equipment. Improving billets	E.B.
do	19-3-19		Preparing new billets for Drivers. checking harness	E.B.
do	20-3-19		Drivers moved from 18 Rue d'Ath to 15 Rue de la Liberté. Improving billets	E.B.
do	21-3-19		Re-arranging wagon park, cleaning vehicles. Inspection of billets by G.O.C. 58th Divl Brigade Group	E.B.
do	22-3-19		Bathing Parade. Rifle inspection. Capt. H. L. Bazalgette returned from Hospital	E.B.
do	23-3-19		Church Parade. 2/Lieut J.L. Fishman transferred to 504th Field Coy R.E.	H.A.
do	24-3-19		Cleaning & oiling vehicles	H.A.

(A7092). Wt. W12839/M1293. 750,000. 1/17. D. D. & L., Ltd. Forms/C.2118/14.

Army Form C. 2118.

Instructions regarding War Diaries and Intelligence Summaries are contained in F. S. Regs., Part II. and the Staff Manual respectively. Title pages will be prepared in manuscript.

WAR DIARY
or
INTELLIGENCE SUMMARY.

(Erase heading not required.)

Place	Date	Hour	Summary of Events and Information	Remarks and references to Appendices
LEUZE	25/3/19		Cleaning & oiling vehicles	
do	26-3-19		Cleaning & oiling vehicles	
do	27-3-19		Work on accommodation	
do	28-3-19		Work on accommodation. Route March	
do	29-3-19		Bathing Parade. Rifle Inspection	
do	30-3-19		Church Parade 343734 Sapper Oates CS. 349056 Sapper Milton WS proceeded to UK for transfer to Regular Army	
do	31-3-19		Double bagging stores. Work on accommodation	

H. J. Baggott Capt

Commanding 503rd (Wessex) Fd. Coy. R.E.

(A7092) Wt. W12839/M1293 75,0 0. 1/17. D. D. & L., Ltd. Forms/C.2118/14.

Army Form C. 2118

WAR DIARY
~~or~~
~~INTELLIGENCE SUMMARY.~~
(Erase heading not required.)

12 52 DW 58

503rd Field Coy RE

Vol 2

Instructions regarding War Diaries and Intelligence Summaries are contained in F. S. Regs., Part II. and the Staff Manual respectively. Title pages will be prepared in manuscript. Ref Map Sheet 44 1/40000

Place	Date	Hour	Summary of Events and Information	Remarks and references to Appendices
LEUZE	1-4-19		Double-bagging Stores. Route March	HLA
do	2-4-19		Double-bagging stores. No 370589 Driver R Blake reported as reinforcement from Etaples Base Depot.	HLA
do	3-4-19		Double-bagging stores. Bathing Parade	HLA
do	4-4-19		Double-bagging stores. 3358602 A/Cpl Fletcher, 217676 Spr Murphy J, 502682 Spr Roden A S, 490348 Spr Smith R, 506539 Spr Sutton F G, 412690 Dr Buchanan J, 370589 Dr Blake R proceeded to join 409th Field Coy RE 1st Division	HLA
do	5-4-19		Route March.	HLA
do	6-4-19		Church Parade	HLA
do	7-4-19		Painting Coy title on vehicles	HLA
do	8-4-19		Route March. Bathing Parade.	HLA
do	9-4-19		Locating Shells at Leuze. Route March.	HLA
do	10-4-19		Excavated 200 shells at Leuze.	HLA
do	11-4-19		Route March	HLA
do	12-4-19		Route March	HLA
do	13-4-19		Church Parade	HLA
do	14-4-19		Route March Bathing Parade.	HLA
do	15-4-19		Inspection of Arms.	HLA
do	16-4-19		Inspection of Kits.	HLA
do	17-4-19		Stencilling Unit title on Vehicles and Stores	HLA

(A7092). Wt W12839/M1293. 75,0 o. 1/17. D. D. & L., Ltd. Forms/C.2118/14.

Instructions regarding War Diaries and Intelligence Summaries are contained in F. S. Regs., Part II. and the Staff Manual respectively. Title pages will be prepared in manuscript.

WAR DIARY
or
INTELLIGENCE SUMMARY.
(Erase heading not required.)

Army Form C. 2118.

503rd Field Coy R.E.

Place	Date	Hour	Summary of Events and Information	Remarks and references to Appendices
LEUZE	18-4-19		No Work.	HLH
do	19-4-19		Changing billets.	HLH
do	20-4-19		Church Parade	HLH
do	21-4-19		No Work.	HLH
do	22-4-19		Cleaning billets Bathing parade	HLH
do	23-4-19		Route March	HLH
do	24-4-19		Route March	HLH
do	25-4-19		Route March	HLH
do	26-4-19		Route March	HLH
do	27-4-19		Church Parade	HLH
do	28-4-19		No Work.	HLH
do	29-4-19		Route March.	HLH
do	30-4-19		No Work Bathing Parade.	HLH

H. J. Hazelgrove[illegible]
Major,
Commanding 503rd (Wessex) Fd. Coy. R.E.

(A7092). Wt W12839/M1293 75,000. 1/17. D. D. & L., Ltd. Forms/C.2118/14.

Instructions regarding War Diaries and Intelligence Summaries are contained in F. S. Regs., Part II. and the Staff Manual respectively. Title pages will be prepared in manuscript.

WAR DIARY
or
~~INTELLIGENCE SUMMARY.~~
(Erase heading not required.)

Army Form C. 2118.

Ref. Map Sheet 44 1/40,000

Place	Date	Hour	Summary of Events and Information	Remarks and references to Appendices
LEUZE	1-5-19		Route March	HLA
do	2-5-19		Work at Divisional Equipment Store	HLA
do	3-5-19		Work at Divisional Equipment Store	HLA
do	4-5-19		Drivers changing billets	HLA
do	5-5-19		Checking Stores at Divisional Equipment Store	HLA
do	6-5-19		Painting vehicles, cleaning and greasing tools	HLA
do	7-5-19		Painting vehicles cleaning and greasing tools	HLA
do	8-5-19		Baths & Fatigues.	HLA
do	9-5-19		Oiling and cleaning vehicles	HLA
do	10-5-19		Oiling and cleaning vehicles	HLA
do	11-5-19		Church Parade	HLA
do	12-5-19		Oiling vehicles	HLA
do	13-5-19		Route march & altering latrines	HLA
do	14-5-19		As yesterday	HLA
do	15-5-19		Baths Fatigues	HLA
do	16-5-19		Route March	HLA
do	17-5-19		Route March	HLA
do	18-5-19		No Parade	HLA

(A7092). Wt W12839/M1293. 75,0 0. 1/17. D. D. & L., Ltd. Forms/C.2118/14.

Army Form C. 2118.

WAR DIARY
or
INTELLIGENCE SUMMARY.
(Erase heading not required.)

Instructions regarding War Diaries and Intelligence Summaries are contained in F. S. Regs., Part II. and the Staff Manual respectively. Title pages will be prepared in manuscript. Ref Map Sheet 44 1/40.000

503rd (WESSEX) No. 1 JUN. 1919 FIELD COY. R.E.

Place	Date	Hour	Summary of Events and Information	Remarks and references to Appendices
LEUZE	19.5.19		Route March & Cleaning Billets	HLA
do	20.5.19		As Yesterday.	HLA
do	21.5.19		As Yesterday.	HLA
do	22.5.19		Baths & Fatigues	HLA
do	23.5.19		Route March	HLA
do	24.5.19		Route March & Cleaning Billets	HLA
do	25.5.19		No Parades	HLA
do	26-5-19		Fatigues	HLA
do	27-5-19		Route March	HLA
do	28-5-19		Route March	HLA
do	29-5-19		Bathing Parade	HLA
do	30-5-19		Fatigues	HLA
do	31-5-19		Fatigues	HLA

[signature] Major,
Commanding 503rd (Wessex) Fd. Coy. R.E.

(A7092). Wt W12839/M1293 75,000. 1/17. D. D. & L., Ltd. Forms/C.2118/14.

www.ingramcontent.com/pod-product-compliance
Lightning Source LLC
Chambersburg PA
CBHW081437160426
43193CB00013B/2310
* 9 7 8 1 4 7 4 5 3 1 0 4 7 *